IN THE PROMISES OF GOD,
I HAVE HOPE

IN THE PROMISES OF GOD,
I HAVE HOPE

Aysha M. Youngblood-Moses
Harry W. Youngblood Jr.

authorHOUSE®

AuthorHouse™
1663 Liberty Drive
Bloomington, IN 47403
www.authorhouse.com
Phone: 1-800-839-8640

© 2012 by Aysha M. Youngblood-Moses & Harry W. Youngblood Jr. All rights reserved.

No part of this book may be reproduced, stored in a retrieval system, or transmitted by any means without the written permission of the author.

Published by AuthorHouse   10/27/2012

ISBN: 978-1-4772-7368-5 (sc)
ISBN: 978-1-4772-7367-8 (hc)
ISBN: 978-1-4772-7366-1 (e)

Library of Congress Control Number: 2012917828

Any people depicted in stock imagery provided by Thinkstock are models, and such images are being used for illustrative purposes only.
Certain stock imagery © Thinkstock.

This book is printed on acid-free paper.

Because of the dynamic nature of the Internet, any web addresses or links contained in this book may have changed since publication and may no longer be valid. The views expressed in this work are solely those of the author and do not necessarily reflect the views of the publisher, and the publisher hereby disclaims any responsibility for them.

CONTENTS

Dedication xi
Acknowledgements xiii
Preface xvii
Scriptures xix

Aysha's Bio xx

Part 1: Aysha's Spiritual Renditions xxi

A: Love and Inspirational Poems xxii

1. Tribute to Mother Marshall 1
2. Our Condolences To The Family of Mother Marshall ... 2
3. What Time Is It? Salvation Time! 3
4. God's Prosperity Path 4
5. A Miracle of Love and Grace 5
6. The Holy Trinity 6
7. Jesus, Lover of My Soul 7
8. My Calling to Service 8
9. A Soldier with the favor of God 10
10. The Gathering of the Saints of God 11
11. Walking in the Light of God 12
12. A New Born Soul 13
13. The Spirit of Unity 14
14. No Regrets 15
15. A Penitent Heart 16
16. I've been in the Storm Too Long 18

17. The Work of the Master's Hand 19
18. Jesus, I Had You to Bring Me Through..................................20
19. Thanksgiving Day Appreciation 21
20. A Family..22
21. Marian Rasool-Hall Home-Going..23
22. Our Mother..24
23. To Our Father 26
24. Just the Two of Us 28
25. The Way We Were..29
26. Like Romeo and Juliet That's How We Were 30
27. My Eternal Love In Memory of Leon Sabatello Jr. 31
28. Vows of Faith and Love 32
29. Renewing Our Vows..33
30. Happy Anniversary..34
31. I Want to Sing to You a Love Song 35
32. The Carnal and Spiritual Battles 36
33. I Can Only Imagine 37
34. In My Solitude 39

B: Inspirational Songs 40

1. I Do It All for Your Glory, So That You Can Have Your Way 41
2. It Won't Be Long..42
3. Open Your Heart unto the Lord 43
4. My Jesus Loves Me, So I Can't Let Go 44
5. The Lord Is My Light and My Salvation..................................45
6. My Faith Looks Up to Thee, Oh lamb of Calvary..................46
7. Lord, I Love You More Each Day 47
8. I'm Coming Up on the Rough Side of the Mountain 48
9. I Want To Go Where Heaven Is...49

10.	I Just Want To Say, Thank You Lord	50
11.	Draw Me Nearer	51
12.	Hold On To God's Hand!	52
13.	The Love of God	53
14.	Peace Like A River	54

Harry's Bio 56

Part 2: Harry's Spiritual Renditions 59

A: Spiritual Poems 60

1.	I Seen Love	61
2.	Crossroads Needmore Road and Needless Road	62
3.	Arise to Love	64
4.	Not Today	65
5.	My Swagga	66
6.	To God in Prayer # 2	67
7.	Sermon Titles	68
8.	Save Me	72
9.	I'm on a Diet	73
10.	He Dried All of My Tears	74
11.	Hospitality	76
12.	Born to Serve	77
13.	Lord, I Thank You for My Life	79
14.	Whispers in the Dark	81
15.	The Thrill is Gone	83
16.	Jehovah is a Rock; I'm a Witness	85
17.	Pastor Miller	86
18.	I Do it All for Your Glory	88
19.	Deacon Johnnie White	89
20.	Frame That Picture	90

21. Legacy 91
22. Remembering Katrina 92
23. ATTITUDES 93
24. Echoes in the Wind 94
25. Real Talk 96
26. I Miss You 97
27. These Hands That I Hold 99
28. In the Promises of God, I Have Hope 100

B: Tribute Poems 102

1. Matriarch . . . . Thinking of you Aunt Dorothy 104
2. Cherish the Love 106
3. A Penny for Your Thoughts 108
4. On the Wings of Love 110
5. A Saint's Graduation Day 113
6. In the Master's Hand 115
7. Purposefully Positioned 117

C: Bonus Section- Poems and Corresponding Sermon Notes 120

Short poems and corresponding notes of messages/spoken word

1. Who Can I Trust? 121
2. You Can Trust In God 122
3. The Life of a Soldier 128
4. A Soldier Story; The Life of a Soldier-Dealing with Adversity 129

Thank You! 139

DEDICATION

I would like to dedicate this book to my Aunt Dorothy Wilburn; a woman that gave so much of herself to so many people. I have many fond memories of you and your spirit is strong with me, I love and miss you dearly but I know that you're in a better place and I'm so glad about that.

Also to Aunt Olivia Smith (affectionately called Aunt Libby); a woman short in stature but strong and tall in the things of God; Holy Ghost filled and fire baptized, she lived a faith filled life blessing the lives of all that she came in contact with and God favored her with her innermost desires.

I have truly been blessed to have these two wonderful women deposit words of life and love into my life and I thank God for the time that He has allowed us to share.

I love you!

ACKNOWLEDGEMENTS

Harry:

The secret to a successful life is having a good relationship with your creator, and I thank God for the relationship that we have now and I look forward to having an even closer one, for in Christ I am traveling into new territory, I'm growing, and I am enjoying my life. I thank God for the talents that He has given me and as I exercise those talents, I am appreciative for the opportunity to once again have materialized in book form the writings from my heart and mind.

To my dad and mom: I thank God for you, I love you and I see myself in the both of you. Thank you for your continued love, inspirations, and encouragements.

To Pastor John Mathis and the Word of Life Ministries: I love you all so much, thank you for your prayers, love, support and at times your listening ear. I'm Godly proud to be in the trenches with you, a ministry that is on the move. We're living life in abundance, to the full, until it overflows.

To my son Tony, my family, and friends: A dream comes forth through a multitude of business and the work has been put in and now the fruits of it will soon be manifested, thank you for your love and support.

To Bishop Anthony Alfred and his wife Renee; thank you for encouraging me down through the years and for having me as the featured poet during your quarterly open mic nights; To the late Bishop Elvin Walker and his wife Pastor Katherine Walker, to Pastors Willie and Robin Little; thank you all for your continued support and encouragement, and for seeing the God in me, you all have blessed my life and I'm eternally grateful.

To John Mathis Jr. thank you for your creative work in designing the book cover for this book, it's funny how it all came to pass but I know that it was nothing but the hand of God.

To Pastor John Mathis and Sis Darcel Coles; thank you for graciously accepting to do a book review for me, I'm greatly appreciative.

To Marcie Hooks; One of Motown's finest! I truly appreciate your spirit and willingness to share your talents, thank you so much for assisting me with your singing on our collaborations.

To Regina Tobe and Franzettai Davis; thank you for your thoughtfulness and efforts in expanding the support of my work.

Aysha:

I give thanks to my Heavenly Father, for my existence and talents to perform the duties of my profession and achieve the goals I have set in my life, until this present time. May I ever be a vessel for his use, to touch the lives of others and assist them in their lives as he has ordained I should do.

PREFACE

In the confines of this book you will find poems that touch on many areas of our lives, along with a confidence in our God that he can supply all of our needs and give us the wisdom to deal with any situation that may arise in our life. Tap into the promises that God have declared, walk in obedience to his word and you shall prosper beyond your wildest imagination. We're on a spiritual journey of love, faith, and hope as we live under an open heaven trusting in our God.

God Bless You!!!

SCRIPTURES

Psalms 90:17 KJV

And let the beauty of the Lord our God be upon us; and establish thou the work of our hands upon us; Yea, the work of our hands establish thou it.

Proverbs 16:3 KJV

Commit thy works unto the Lord and thy thoughts shall be established.

Aysha Marie Youngblood-Moses Bio

I, Aysha Youngblood-Moses was born in Pittsburgh, Pennsylvania on August 20, 1935; I attended grade school and high school there. I married and gave birth to two children there before moving to Chicago, Illinois where my other children were born. I attended Lake College and Bryant and Stratton Business College. I was a student of LaSalle University and of Twentieth Century Bible College, among other educational courses of study for the positions held. I am an ordained minister; entrepreneur, great grandmother, former foster mother, and educational surrogate parent for special education children, former certified nurse assistant, attending handicapped children and home bound senior citizens, tutor for adults and children. My hobbies and interests: piano, organ, singing, writing (songs, poems, and greetings for all occasions), swimming, basketball, baseball, movies, some video games, and I compose newsletters with inspirational messages. I presently reside in Clarksville, Tennessee.

PART 1:
AYSHA'S SPIRITUAL RENDITIONS

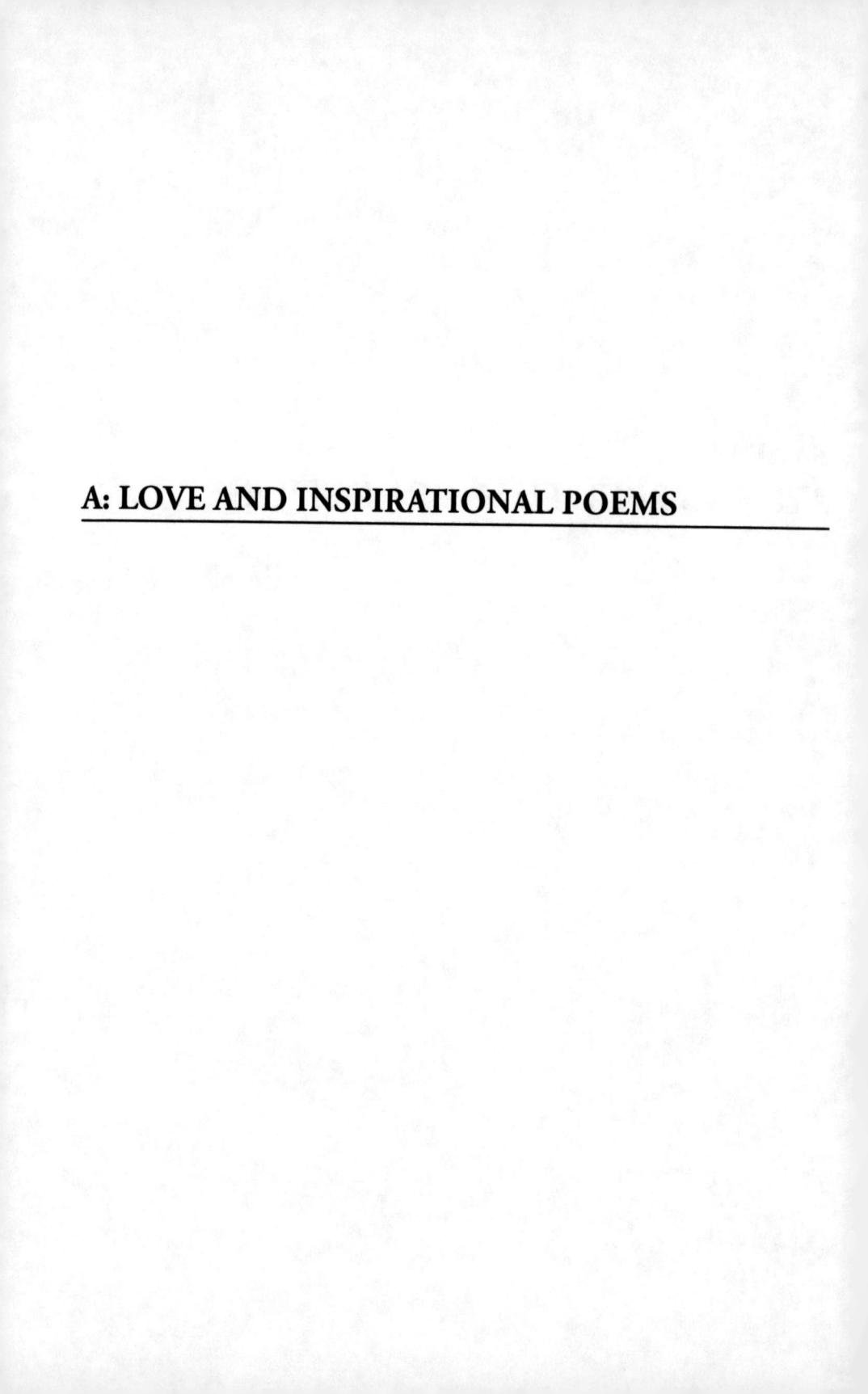

A: LOVE AND INSPIRATIONAL POEMS

TRIBUTE TO MOTHER MARSHALL

(A person of a sweet and quiet spirit)
Home-Going Service July 30, 2009

Blessed quietness, holy quietness, what assurance in my soul,
When life's stormy sea, toss and shifts me, Jesus speaks to me
And the storm waves cease to roll.

Mother Marshall, as I can testify to, for the length of time I have known her,
Was a sweet and quiet person, until she felt!
The presence of God, then you would hear her praising Him,
I enjoyed our brief moments of greeting each other and worshipping
Our Heavenly Father and our Savior, and I thought of her often,
And I remembered her in my prayers, in between the days of church services.

I believe she, as do I, looked forward to seeing our Savior's face,
After our warfare here on earth, in that heavenly place;
Free from sickness and sorrow, in that sweet home on tomorrow,
Eager to hear His voice, cares all past, in our eternal home at last,
Forever to rejoice!

It behooves you and me, to make our calling and election for His divine
Service of the greatest effect, so when next on the roll is called,
Your name or mine He may select, to enter those gates of gold
Where we'll never die or ever have to say goodbye.

I await to worship and praise the Lord with her again, it will be a treat,
To be surrounded by others, Saints and Angels, near our Savior's seat.
Amen!

OUR CONDOLENCES
TO THE FAMILY OF MOTHER MARSHALL

May the Lord grant you His peace that passes human understanding!
During this time of your sorrow,
May He grant you His joy which is unspeakable for hope of tomorrow!

Remembering happy days gone by
With your loved one who is now on high,
Expecting to see all of you with her by the Savior's side!

Resolve to be all that God wants you to be,
Working for His Kingdom continuously;

So when your life comes to a close,
Happily you can go to be with her and our Savior in sweet repose.

May the Lord be with you and you with His Spirit!   Amen!

WHAT TIME IS IT?
SALVATION TIME!

Time and time again, it never seems to end
Someone asks the question, "what time is it?"
One may say, "Its break time!" while another one says, "It's my time!"
Still another one says, "Its nation time!", but for sure, "Its salvation time!"

What time is it? Salvation time! What time is it? Salvation time!
What are you going to do? Open my mind, my body, my spirit;
Why? For the renewing of my mind, the cleansing of my body,
And it's for the union of the Holy Ghost and my spirit in it.

What time is it? Salvation time! What time is it? Salvation time!
Why? For the heavenly places are holy and all that are sanctified, it is reserved for them only.

Tell me! What time is it?   Salvation time! What time is it? Nation time!
What time is it? Preparation time! What time is it? Going home time!
Church! Get ready to go, don't be too slow, because our Bridegroom is on the way
So make haste, and don't you stray from the narrow path
Time is too short and there is too much to gain, at the break of dawn, that day.
Be strong and true, no matter what others do, don't evoke the Father's wrath.

Teach others to do the same, so they too may dwell peaceably in the land of tomorrow.
Praising Jesus holy name, with the Saints and Angels proclaiming victory,
Over sin and Satan, enjoying peace, love, and unity instead of sorrow.

GOD'S PROSPERITY PATH

Seasons come and seasons go, in these latter days,
One from another is hard to be known
And so it is within this spiritual realm.
You can speculate by interjection of thought,
But you only know for sure when it has been shown.
Many will tell you to look for one thing or another,
To know the working of God
But in most instances one may say, why bother?
Because at the appointed time, the Holy Spirit will reveal
All things pertaining to our life upon this earthly sod,
The word of God tells us to be content in whatever state we're in.
Standing firmly on the promises of God, with faith in our hearts,
Being thankful for each day's supply
Upon the faithfulness of our Heavenly Father rely.
Knowing all we ask in Jesus name, for our needs and even our desires
Will be given, as we live in praise unto the Lord;
Thanking the Lord for all he has done and never get tired,
Witnessing when the opportunity arises and cutting asunder
All evil with our mighty sword,
So you don't kindle our Heavenly Father's wrath,
Travel only in God's prosperity path.

A MIRACLE OF LOVE AND GRACE

It took a miracle to put the stars in space,
It took a miracle to form the human race.
It took a miracle for everything to be,
It took a miracle of love and grace.

It took a miracle to form salvation's plan,
It took a miracle, by the blood of the Holy Lamb.
It took a miracle of birth, for you and me,
It took a miracle of love and grace to be.

It took a miracle to show God's healing power,
It took a miracle to witness, hour by hour.
It took some miracles for men to believe,
Still it takes miracles of love and grace, you see.

It took a miracle to free the Hebrew slaves,
It took a miracle to stay the Pharaoh's hand.
It took a miracle to feed their craves,
It was a miracle of love and grace, in that desert land.

THE HOLY TRINITY

One of the greatest mysteries to mankind is the God-head,
Many believe in the Holy Trinity, while others believe in the Father.
The word of God plainly states there are three entities,
But various denominations teach the other belief instead.
We hold this truth evident, that at the time of creation of all things,
There existed the three.
The Father, Jesus; his son, and the Holy Ghost, who as one agreed,
That all there was and all there will be would be brought into harmony,
This was and still is God's plan.
From the beginning of time, until these latter days,
The visitation of angels heralded God's message, throughout the land.
The Apostles preached his word and manifested his power in many ways.
God's word states that we should believe him, instead of men,
We should come into harmony with those of all nations and living without sin.
We should shun evil and cleave unto that, which is pure,
Make our election or calling to whatever service, sure.
Our Heavenly Father, was the primary teacher for his chosen ones, the Israelites,
Jesus; his son, was the primary teacher, during the early Christian era.
Before the ascension, Jesus told his disciples that the Holy Ghost was coming,
In which they were not aware of.
At the time the Holy Ghost was given, the Apostles and other disciples were
transformed and empowered by his teaching,
Speaking through them, in other languages, as a witness to those they were reaching;
The message of faith, love, and harmony has transformed many and me,
As it has come through the ranks of our civilization, with a profound revelation;
That God the Father, God the Son, and God the Holy Ghost are the Holy Trinity.

JESUS, LOVER OF MY SOUL

When I was lost in a world of sin,
In the midst of many who had no hope and empty within;
At home, I was not taught that Jesus died for me,
Arose from the dead, so empowered I could be.

Then according to God's plan,
A Sister of Charity taught me about Jesus and I began to understand;
How our Heavenly Father loved his creation so, that he gave his only son,
For a world of sinners, just like me, through faith we could become one.

Over the years, I've grown to care,
More and more, while a wealth of knowledge we share;
Communicating words of affection, and guiding me by the precious Holy Ghost,
Unveiling promises foretold; that's why I love him the most.

Jesus, lover of my soul,
I am so grateful; you have saved me and made my body whole,
Against the evil forces you have empowered me,
To live victoriously, here on earth, and the hereafter, to be with thee;

Jesus, lover of my soul,
Your loving image, I desire to behold;
Immersed in your warm embrace,
After I have run this race;
Clothed with immortality, adorned for royalty,
Presented with a heavenly role;
To you, Jesus; lover of my soul,
Amen!

MY CALLING TO SERVICE
(For Sis Elizabeth Person)

Oh, how sweet to trust in Jesus, just to take Him at His word,
Just in simple faith to trust Him, in all that we have seen and heard.
Jesus, how I trust you, how I have proved you over and over again,
Morning, noon, night, no matter the hour or the day, it was then.

Faith rooted in your word, which is the truth
Abounding in love and righteousness,
Striving to be faultless, though the evil one doesn't tempt me any less,
My hope is built on nothing less, than Jesus, the solid rock upon which I stand.
Because all other ground is sinking sand, and I dare not trust the sweetest sensation,
But hold firmly, to my God-given invitation and assume the attached obligation.

For this cause, I do affirm, that I am His and He is mine, forever more
His love for me has been shown in many ways, and words cannot tell, how much Him I adore.
I do not know what I would be, if it had not been for His love, shown to me,
So full of gloom and misery, my life was, until the day I realized my need for him, and
He set me free, then the call to become an end-time messenger of the truth, enlightened
And empowered by the precious Holy Ghost, to do all that is commanded of me!

I will continue this daily quest to be of service to the Saints of God and the strangers,
Within the gate, standing in the gap between Heaven and Hell, fighting on their behalf,
While awaiting their fate, Oh what joy will fill my soul when at the last trumpet sound,
And my blessed Lord's face to behold, with love and peace all around!

Let it be known this day, I'm going to stay in the holy way, according to my calling to service, While in my youth, now I'm no longer a novice; but a seasoned warrior of God,
Going here and there, throughout this earthly sod, purposed to work for Him,
Until my name, from the roll of Heaven is called, when these weary eyes grow dim;
As the veil of life close and I will be in sweet repose. Amen!

A SOLDIER WITH THE FAVOR OF GOD

Once there was a shepherd boy, chosen by God and anointed by his prophet,
A humble child, who loved and worshipped God;
To honor, obey, and to be pleasing to God, is how his mind was set,
And this is why, according to the scripture, he was called, "the apple of God's eye"
Enjoying the blessing of God and being chastened by his rod.

During the course of his life, and before the kingly reign,
He grew into an honorable man and became acquainted with pain;
But the Lord upheld him, by his mighty hand,
And let it be known, without a doubt, that he was God's man.

When the time came, for him to receive the crown,
The Lord had given him many victories in war, and a name of renown;
King Saul sought to kill him, to keep him from the throne,
But his plan did not succeed, as in the scriptures we read, Saul's reign was overthrown.

Clearly, a soldier with the favor of God, no one could dispute his fame,
Loved by God's people and God's prophet as well,
Much was accomplished for the children of Israel, through the authority of his name,
As the books of Kings, his story tell,
To this man of valor, we give the nod,
King David of Israel, a soldier with the favor of God;
Amen!

THE GATHERING OF THE SAINTS OF GOD

One day very soon upon this earthly sod,
All will seem calm, but a stirring by the precious Holy Ghost,
Will cause a gathering of the Saints of God;
No one knows when, where, or what hour, it will occur,
But this event will take place, and that's for sure.

Some will be at work, while others will be somewhere alone,
And yet, there may be others, who can't be reached by phone;
Individually or collectively shopping in the store,
The hustle or bustle of people that day will seem to be much more.

Some people will cry out like an alarm,
Wondering if their loved ones have met some form of harm;
As they look everywhere and none of them can be found,
This wondrous event will cause confusion without an audible sound.

Oh what joy there will be, when the Savior's face they see!
Troubles of their lives will be just a memory;
There should be no complaints,
When there's a gathering of the Saints.
As they are transformed supernaturally;
To fight the greatest battle there will ever be,
Then to be mustered for the journey to their eternal home,
Where they will live forever; never more to roam!

WALKING IN THE LIGHT OF GOD

In the midst of confusion and chaos everywhere,
I am content, having peace and joy within.
Surrounded by those who wander and they stare,
Not knowing that it's because I've been born again.

Years before I knew the Lord, there was only darkness,
Engulfed by all that was unholy;
But now I'm grateful and mightily blessed,
To be walking in the light of God and solely.

Words can't express the joy that floods my soul,
As I go along life's way.
But be it known to all, far and near, by the Holy Spirit I am bold,
And I am steadfast upon the promises of God each day.

Walking in the light of God,
As I move throughout this earthly sod.
No matter what comes to hinder me,
To my Heavenly Father and my Savior, I will faithfully be.
Amen! Praise to Them!

A NEW BORN SOUL

When I was a teenager many years ago,
The path of holiness and the process of transformation
I didn't know.

But being led by the Holy Spirit, to one who played a special spiritual role,
My eyes were made to see and my ears were made to hear spiritually,
What the Holy Spirit witnessed to me.
With an open mind and a receptive heart, a sincere prayer of repentance,
From my lips, I became a new born soul.

Then I knew what our Heavenly Father required for salvation,
Not a mere form of worship, like I had believed
But a committed life with a full transformation,
From inherited and committed sins, a worthy witness of God,
By the world could be received.

A staunch advocate for God's Word and His way,
Eager to do or to go, as the Lord leads each day;
Thoughtful and concerned about others,
He entreated those of all nations, with respect and as brothers.

When the veil of life has closed and these eyes no longer see,
I can be assured the Lord will welcome me.
He will escort me to live in his holy place for eternity.

THE SPIRIT OF UNITY

How sweet it is for brethren to dwell together in the spirit of unity,
A union made by our Heavenly Father, between the Holy Ghost, brethren around the world and me,
All of us make up the bride of Jesus Christ, our Savior.
Purchased by his precious blood, having the Heavenly Father's favor
Dwelling in this sinful world, we must labor.
For the cause of Christ and our salvation,
We're fighting against the evil forces while representing Jesus in our nation.
Putting aside the prejudices, denominational stigmas, classifications, and segregation,
We must emerge in victory, for the Lord's name sake.
Holding up the blood-stained banner of the Lord as we go,
Showing to the world the reality of a born again soul as the Word of God says so,
In our hearts let the Word of God be true.
Let our lights of righteousness shine through,
Refusing to live like sinful men do,
Pressing toward the mark of the high calling set by God,
our heavenly reward we pursue.
Let all the brethren hear, who have ears to hear,
What the Holy Ghost is saying so loud and clear.
For the hope of humanity depends on our loyalty,
Being the holy bride of royalty,
Hold fast to your faith, as we run this race.
Let no one deter you until we see our Savior, face to face.
Praise him every time you get a chance,
Let the world know of this sweet romance,
And testify of his goodness and warm embrace.

NO REGRETS

Isn't it good, at the end of the day?
To look towards heaven and say,
During the course of my day
I was able to be of help to someone along the way.

But it would be sad, if you must say,
That I hurt my brother or sister in some way,
So as you do your job assigned to you
Remember that you are your brother's keeper too.

What good you can do for them, don't fail to give,
By this token of love and concern you must live.
To have our Heavenly Father's mercy and care,
Be bestowed upon you, knowingly or unaware.

To love one another, as the Lord has loved us,
It is a duty of the Children of God, in whom they trust.
Remembering that the good that we sow unto men,
It shall be reaped in kind, by us again.

A PENITENT HEART

Oh, the blood of Jesus! Oh, the blood of Jesus! Oh, the blood of Jesus!
It washes white as snow.
Many times in the past I have heard this song, but it was not until this moment,
That I felt guilty of doing any wrong,
Like a mirror on the wall, reflecting what is in view, tells it all;
Memories of my past cloud my mind, leaving nothing out that is of an evil kind.

Oh Lord, of what manner we mortals are, formed in sin to live therein,
Because that was our destiny;
My life has been one of pain and misery, though I played a part of one whom,
Had peace and was very happy;

Spiritually I was so blind, the meaning of your word I could not understand,
Until now I didn't know if I should go left or right,
But now is the beginning of a brand new day.
Because you have heard my plea,
And you have come to rescue me from the darkness of sin,
And I'm no longer to live therein, because of your marvelous light.

I recall the time when I heard the saints sing,
"Don't let it be said too late, to enter Heaven's gate."
The farthest thought from my mind,
Now on the brink of destruction, the path that I should take is in view,
With a shout of exclamation, and heartfelt adoration, I partake of a life sublime
And leave a life of sin behind.

Be it known this day, the garments of righteousness I adorn,
A rightful heir to the promises of God, through the blood of Jesus,
Again, I have been born. Amen!

I'VE BEEN IN THE STORM TOO LONG

Oh Lord! The storm winds are raging upon life's tumultuous sea,
As in bible days long ago, when Peter cried, "Lord help me!"
Similar waves o'er me roll, as I'm tossed to and fro, gasping for air,
As did the disciples, I know you love me so much.
And that whatever befalls me, you care,
But Lord, I've been in the storm too long!

Knowing the evil forces desire my demise and await a horrible fate,
I'm assured by your word and events of the past; you are never too late,
Lord, you know my heart and the thoughts of my mind.
Only you know the course I take and what lies ahead,
But my emotions are enhanced and my bodily functions unwind,
As I sink into oblivion, a watery tomb is in view,
But memories of your grace, in the past cause me to focus on you instead.
Yet I cry, Lord, I've been in the storm too long!

Let it be dear Lord, just let it be,
Thou know what is best for me.
Thy art the potter and I'm just the clay,
Mold and make me, after thine own way.
Soon in the midst of the deep, I feel your presence engulfing me,
Your warm embrace, like no other to be compared, brings into sync body, mind,
And spirit; as you lift me to a place of safety.
Still I cry, Lord, I've been in the storm too long!

THE WORK OF THE MASTER'S HAND

Out of darkness, and within His sight,
God, our Heavenly Father, brought forth the sun, moon, and stars,
With their marvelous light,
The matter was separated from the water, the earth and seas came into being.
According to his plan,
Introducing mysteries and miracles by the Master's hand!

He took matter mixed with water and life's energy force from Himself,
And created mankind,
All of the animals, the fouls of the air, the fish in the rivers and seas,
Formed and fashioned by His design.
This is how everything there is and all you see came to be.
These intricate, skillful works, unique within themselves,
Individually and corporally aligned,
From the Master's hand and His creative mind!

What other mastery of thought or deed, performed by men on earth,
Could match the miraculous feats of an infinite entity,
None are known whose works can compare to those of our Heavenly Father!
Whose creations span from the heavenly elements, humanity and all things of worth.
Although there be those who try to compete through their wisdom,
in this chaotic land,
Try as they may, from now until judgment day their achievements will
pale in the light,
And of the wondrous works of the Master's hand.

JESUS, I HAD YOU TO BRING ME THROUGH

I never would have made it without you,
The toils, snares, and every day cares
Wore me down, unable to utter a sound too,
Because I lack the energy and confusion of mind,
This hindered the process of sync as I was caught unaware.

Woe is me, a wretch undone mete for an untimely end,
This was my thought until you came and set me free.
A victim of the curse imposed upon Adam and Eve,
A perpetrator in my own right, by the blood of Jesus, I am forgiven.
Jesus, I had you to bring me through!

No one else could do what was needed to be done,
Though there were friends, relatives, associates, even daughters and sons.
It took you, the Son of God, the only perfect one,
By God's grace, love, and power to join my body, mind, and spirit,
with His again, into a holy union.
Jesus, I had you to bring me through! Only you could do what you do.

Yet a while before the veil of life closes upon the events of many years,
Still the evil forces lurk seeking opportunity to offend and hinder me.
But I am determined to stand firm on the Word of God and Jesus,
The solid rock and corner stone of the house not built by hand.
Eagerly waiting to enter the Promised Land, then I can say to Him,
Jesus, I had you to bring me through!

THANKSGIVING DAY APPRECIATION

Lord, I just want to say, "Thank You!"
You've been so good to me, opening doors which I could not see,
In my life and for the salvation of others, you gave the victory.

You've been with me through the years,
Putting joy and peace in place of my fears;
Throughout the turmoil and rubble, you let me find those who are my brethren,
And you rescued me out of my trouble.

For these and many other blessings received is why I must say "Thank You Lord!"
Along life's way, but especially on Thanksgiving Day!

A FAMILY

This is what "A Family" means to me,
A group of people related to each other,
By blood or marriage, sister or brother,
Aunts and uncles, and cousins alike dedicated to the welfare of one another.
If one is hungry, by another he'll be fed,
Closely knitted together, in the spirit of harmony,
One for all, and all for one, is the motto by which they are sustained.
And orderly led firmly, grounded in love, they will forever be.
What troubles you, troubles me,
When you are glad, I am happy.
You have problems; the rest of us will help to solve them.
For this is the commandment of the Lord, and we do all to honor him.
The family that prays together, stays together is the truth!
Because we are "A Family" manifesting the proof,
Come what may, from day to day, you will hear us say,
Flesh of my flesh, bone of my bone, joined in every way,
Strengthened by the power of God, by the gospel peace, our feet are shod.
We are as one, with each other, perfect unity,
And by fusion of spirits, with the blessed Trinity,
All of this and more is what "A Family" should be.

MARIAN RASOOL-HALL HOME-GOING
(Mother of Aysha M. Youngblood-Moses)

A blessed event arranged by our Heavenly Father,
Because of His loving kindness and tender mercy,
Recaptured the breath for living, and left her in sweet repose, amidst the others.

She spent her life as best she could, and there was no need in this world to go further,
So our Heavenly Father according to His plan, caused to cease her pain and misery,
And now remains in our hearts and minds, all the former and present memories shared, with one another.

A woman slow to speak and slow to anger, her daily life was mostly free from strife,
But now in the calmness of a darkened plane of existence, she can look forward to the promise of peace, joy, and happiness in an Eternal Life.

Oh what joy to see His face, the one who has kept her by His grace,
Cares of the world all past, entering her Eternal Home at last.
Amidst the Heavenly Host, our Heavenly Father, Jesus our Savior, and the precious Holy Ghost!

A former Muslim who became a born-again child of God,
Showed respect for her elders and others as she walked this earthly sod.
Friendly and kind with a code of ethics in mind,
She lived by the Golden Rule and the Word of God.

OUR MOTHER
(God's Gift of Love to Others and Us)

Our mother, God's gift of love to others and us,
Certainly it's a fact our Heavenly Father and our mother are the ones we trust.
There is no secret what God can do and surely it is known what our mother does too,
As she fills her days with loving care, for us and others who come to her on any day.
And parting with "God be with you!"

Because God is love and she is a part of Him,
Love is emitted from her to us and others, in many different forms throughout the day.
When we think to praise the Lord for all His goodness and blessings,
We must include our mother, for she is one of the best of them.
Most of all of what our mother is to us and others, she exhibits the kind of love which,
Goes from heart to heart and is shared one with another, as they go along life's way.

Yes, our mother is the ultimate example of the manifestation of love in everything,
She says and does for us and others.
Having no respect of persons, she will help and pray for everyone, who has a desire or need,
Because the bible says that we are sisters and brothers.
She prays for us and others every day and night,
Asking the Lord's guidance and for his power to aid us, in our spiritual warfare,
Just to make everything alright.

She calls every now and then to find out what's going on and if we are well,
And though we don't always tell her everything, somehow she can tell.
She encourages our dreams as though they were her own,
She gives us and others her best advice, speaking in a loving tone.
Invoking love, peace, and harmony, imparting hope in times of despair,
Filling our spirits with joy, as she tells of her spiritual victories;
It builds our faith and increases our determination to be victorious warriors too,
So we can tell our wondrous stories.

TO OUR FATHER
Harry Wesley Youngblood Sr.
June 15, 2008

A father fair, a father true

A caring and loving one who did for us, no one else would do.

You took us to the park and we played to almost dark,

We played ball and board games, when you had the time to share,

You showed concern and love for us, making it easy for us to show how much we care.

A father not like many others,

Bonded together with your sons and daughters, like many sisters and brothers.

You gave of yourself for us, even to the point of sacrifice,

We didn't realize it then as much as we do now, how great a price.

Down through the years during the time we have been apart,

Fond memories of you lingered, and the love remained in our hearts.

We know now more than we knew then,

How difficult your struggle was and we prayed that you would win.

You deserved more than fate allowed, and to do all to make you happy is our vow,

Now that you are in the twilight years,

Call upon us, when you need help for you are not alone, have no fears.

You have stood by us; allow us to stand by you,
To be caring and loving is what we want to do.
So rest in assurance, you are loved as you should be,
And there is no one who could love you more than your family.

This is why we send laurels and give you honor when we say,
Have a blessed and wonderful Father's Day!

JUST THE TWO OF US

Just the two of us, we'll make it to the top,
Just the two of us, Satan and his entire host cannot stop.
All up above are yours and mine,
Happy together throughout time,
Just the two of us! Just the two of us!

Just the two of us, through Jesus blood we've been reborn,
Just the two of us, we'll be lifted up at the sound of Gabriel's horn.
Praising the Lord, so glad to be home,
Singing with the Heavenly Choir, never more to roam,
Just the two of us! Just the two of us!

Just the two of us, we'll be there when Jesus is crowned,
King of Kings and Lord of Lords,
Just the two of us in the midst of the Saints and Angels forming a magnificent hoard;
Raising our voices in exclamation,
With love and devotion; along with others of different nations,
Just the two of us! With the rest of us!

THE WAY WE WERE

Memories! Flood the corners of my mind,
Misty water-colored memories of the way we were.
Precious pictures of the times we used to share,
Priceless moments that we cherished, because of our love affair;
Was it because it was all so simple then, or has time rewritten every line?
If we had the chance to do it all again, tell me, would we? Could we?
Make our lives so sublime, as in earlier times.
Feelings! For those days, so long ago,
Smoldering, haunting, lingering feelings, I can't let go;
Some days we lived to regret,
What's too painful to remember, we chose to forget?
But now with laughter, we will remember, for we'll live happily ever after,
Remembering the way we were. The way we were.

LIKE ROMEO AND JULIET THAT'S HOW WE WERE

My Leo, the one I love the most, the one who means so very much to me,
And when he is near, my heart begins to beat so rapidly, I can't conceive my thoughts.
Like Romeo and Juliet, that's how we were.

My Leo, a sweet and mild-mannered man, I longed to e within his warm embrace,
To feel the touch of his lips, in a gentle loving kiss, wrapped in his arms.
Those precious moments time cannot erase, like Romeo and Juliet, that's how we were.

Down through the years, before we met, I would day-dream about such a lover,
Cinderella, Romeo and Juliet were stories I favored and soon a love like theirs I would discover.
Many times in the course of your life, you hope and pray that your dreams come true,
But I never thought I could have such a love like theirs, no matter what I would do.

I have known a love so strong and true, from a man so kind and faithful,
So thoughtful and unselfish, a gentleman in every way,
How could I help but to show him love and affection in return, and to God, be ever so grateful.

But as in the stories, evil forces were at work to come against us,
To try to break the bond of love and trust;
And though they succeeded through physical separation,
Time, hardships, and others could not dissolve that love affair, strengthened by precious memories and a strong determination.
Like Romeo and Juliet, that's how we were.

MY ETERNAL LOVE
IN MEMORY OF LEON SABATELLO JR.

Darling, if we never meet again,
My darling, before my lifetime ends;
I want you to know, I've loved you only,
These years without you, have been so lonely.

Remember the day that you and I,
Embraced before a flaming fire;
You told me to vow to never leave you,
I tried not to, didn't I? Though, time proved me a liar.

Since we can't be together,
My life in this world no longer matters.
I'm yours alone forever and ever,
No one else will have my love, no never.

My love, my love, my eternal love!

My eternal love and I had a love affair,
With others, it could not be compared.
A special union of heart, mind, and spirit,
Combined with joy and satisfaction,
Having to fight for what was right for us.

There was nothing to it,
Possessing strong wills and mindsets,
Strengthened our determination without distraction;
Though years may come and go, this we will always know,
Wherever we may be, I am his true and everlasting love, as he is to me.

VOWS OF FAITH AND LOVE

In the presence of almighty God we stand,
Humbly and joyfully hand in hand,
We acknowledge God's written plan.

Hearts aglow, with love for each other we know,
We vow to love, honor, and to be faithful also,
Believing in times of weakness, God's power will be bestowed.

We pray, that our Heavenly Father will guard us along life's way,
Leading us into paths of righteousness, guiding us through the darkest vale,
He upholds us with his mighty hands, as we fight against the hordes of hell.
So with love, peace, and joy as our foundation,
We will go forth proclaiming freedom of mind, body, and spirit,
To all people of every nation, according to the Holy Writ!
Amen!

RENEWING OUR VOWS

Once again we come to you dear Lord, as humbly as we know how,
To ask for forgiveness for weaknesses of the past;
Seeking your grace, as we make anew our vows,
To love, honor, and cherish each other for as long as our lives shall last.

Enlighten us, in the way we should go, and how we should be,
Enrich our lives with peace, joy, and harmony.
Until the appointed time when we must be with thee,
To be transported from this earthly sod, to a Heavenly Place, for eternity.

May our spirits be entwined with thy precious Holy Ghost!
To be wholly thine in every way, is what we want the most.
Let us be a testimony of thy Word and of thy Power,
To all we meet each day and every hour.

Safe and secure within your loving arms,
Direct and guard us from harm.
Over sin and Satan, give us victory,
So when the trumpet sounds, in your presence we will ever be.
Amen!

HAPPY ANNIVERSARY

Happy Anniversary! My dear,
It has been so nice having you so near.
The first thing I see each day,
Feeling your arms around me and the warmth of your smile,
As I leave for work I'll be thinking of you along the way.
Memories of the times we've spent will be in my thoughts for a while.

We have weathered the storms of life throughout the year,
Holding on to our faith and the power of God, we've had no fear.
Knowing we are assured of victory over the evil one,
Through our Lord and Savior Jesus Christ, God's only son;
So onward we go, down the straight and narrow path,
And we will defeat all enemies, leaving nothing but the aftermath.

With Love in our hearts, eyes aglow, unified in spirit, no sorrow we'll know,
As we press our way through the labyrinth of life.
Love, Peace, and Harmony in our lives will only show,
By this time, another year has gone past, because of God's grace upon this husband and wife.

I WANT TO SING TO YOU A LOVE SONG

I've been loving you so long, it doesn't matter what has happened that was wrong,
Pain and misery mostly is all I've known, while being alone;
Beats of my heart began to pound, as loving thoughts of you go round and round,
So rapidly, in a chaotic state it leaves me.

The one I've loved the most, visions of you haunt me like a friendly ghost,
Memories of the past invade my present state, making it difficult to concentrate,
On anything, or anyone, but you, Honey it's true, and as long as breath remain within.
The cavity of this fleshly frame, I believe this to be my destiny and my only claim to fame,
I've loved and I have been loved by a man once.

But oh, what yonder breaks the opening of Love's Gate,
Beckoning us to come inside, where forever, we can hide,
And once again we can enjoy all there is within.
Until the veil of death overshadows us and the book of our lives close,
Rendering us in sweet repose to live together with those in Heaven.

THE CARNAL AND SPIRITUAL BATTLES

There are two battles we face from day to day,
One of the flesh, and the other of the spirit realm along the Christian Way!

For both, we must be fortified with strength, knowledge, gear, and weaponry,
If we are to enjoy the Father's favor and our ultimate victory!

So forward into battle with the blood-stained banner raised,
We will lift our voice, with a mighty cry of Hallelujah! Our highest form of praise!

Since the battles are not ours but the Lords,
There is still something we must do against the evil hordes.

We must listen for the Lord's voice, so that we will be able to make the right choice,
In making decisions and strengthening our lines of force.

I CAN ONLY IMAGINE

I can only imagine how Jesus felt, when the soldiers and Judas entered the garden to take Him to the prison,

I can only imagine how Jesus felt, when he was accused, beaten, and his head held a crown of thorns.

I can only imagine how Jesus felt, when he was nailed to the cross, bled, and died for the salvation of mankind, and the third day was risen.

I can only imagine how Jesus felt, when he saw the doubt in Thomas eyes and the rest of the disciples amazed and forlorn.

I can only imagine how Jesus felt, as he looked upon those fleshly bodies filled with despair and confusion as He told them to go and wait for the Holy Ghost,

I can only imagine how Jesus felt, as they beheld Him, as He ascended into the air;

I can only imagine how Jesus felt, as He watched their tear-glazed eyes holding Him within their sights, knowing their disappointment because He could not remain with them there.

But with the coming of the Holy Ghost, everything changed and eyes perceived, Ears began to hear, and to eager awaiting hearts, the answers of this mystery were revealed.

Until this present time, when as a seeker of truth, the answers were imparted into my heart, and by the Holy Ghost, sealed;

Now I can tell you how Jesus felt, because of the clarity within me,
He felt so much compassion for mankind despite their sinful state, and He loved them enough to pay the price so that they could be free. Amen!

Now there's no need to imagine! (Repeat 2 times)

IN MY SOLITUDE

In my solitude, various situations and conditions weigh heavily upon me,
These problems of others for which I cry out to the Lord daily;
Sounds of trouble all around, heartache and pain on the upward bound,
They invade my peaceful state of mind while in my solitude.

Oh what wretched ones there be, within my homeland and across the sea,
Ever beckoning to others as well as to me;
Help us if you can, we need your helping hand,
Food banks and shelters are doing their best,
But what about those who have plenty to eat and fancy homes wherein they rest;

Many of these people have no qualms concerning the needs of others,
Because they don't see them as their sisters and brothers;
Oh what foolish creatures these be, having eyes but cannot see,
The value of human life they have not learned, the cries for help they have spurned.
In things of the world they are astute seeking all kinds of tribute,
Squandering their money on frivolous things and so called "hot honeys"
These things and more affect my mood while in my solitude.

I await the time of my prosperity, as promised by the Lord in sincerity,
To have more than enough for me, then I can share my wealth with the least fortunate few.
Dwelling around me of which I think about and pray for in my solitude.

B: INSPIRATIONAL SONGS

I DO IT ALL FOR YOUR GLORY, SO THAT YOU CAN HAVE YOUR WAY

Verse 1

I do it all for your glory, so that you can have your way,
I do it all for your glory, so that your name can be praised.
For your glory, I do it, so that others can know your fame,
For your glory, I do it, so that your power they will proclaim.

Chorus:

Have your way, today, in this place,
Have your way, today, in this place,
I do it all for your glory, so that I can see your face.

Verse 2

I do it all for your glory, in everything day to day,
I do it all for your glory, to have your favor when I pray.
For your glory, I do it, to get a glimpse of Heaven's rays,
For your glory, I do it, and will continue 'til the end of my days.

Verse 3

I do it all for your glory, feeling you near me, hour by hour
I do it all for your glory, strengthen by your mighty power.
For your glory, I do it, 'til the victory is won,
For your glory, I do it, then I will hear you say, well done.

IT WON'T BE LONG

Verse 1

Jesus is coming back again, to receive those saved from sin,
He will not tarry, no not long, you'll not have time to right any wrong. Oh, Glory!
Hallelujah! It won't be long.

Verse 2

A few more days to labor and wait, until we enter Heaven's Gate,
There we shall shout and praise the Lord, everyone in sweet accord.
Oh, Glory! Hallelujah! It won't be long.

Verse 3

Time then on earth, will be done; victory will have been won,
The sun will refuse to shine; all in Heaven will be mine.
Oh, Glory! Hallelujah! It won't be long.

Chorus

Lead: No, it won't be long
Background: It won't be long
Lead: Not very long
Background: Not very long
Lead: It won't be long, to see his face, who has kept us by his grace,
    Oh, yes, what a day! It won't be long.
Background: It won't be long   (Repeat 1 time)

OPEN YOUR HEART UNTO THE LORD

Verse 1

When your burdens seem so hard to bear,
And there's not one who seems to care,
Remember Jesus is aware,
So open your heart unto the Lord

Verse 2

When there are those who tend to treat you wrong,
And everything you do seem to fail,
Jesus will make you strong,
He'll calm all your life's Gales.
So open your heart unto the Lord.

Chorus

Lead: he will come into your heart

Background: into your heart, into your heart

Lead: if you let him, oh yes, He will come into your heart

Background: into your heart, into your heart

Lead: take away all of your sin, He will come into your life

Background: into your heart, into your heart

Lead: take away all confusion and strife, if you just let him, Jesus will come in and abide.

MY JESUS LOVES ME, SO I CAN'T LET GO

Verse 1: I almost gave up; life had given me such a bitter cup,
Troubles had me bound, confusion was all around.

Chorus: But Jesus said "No! Don't let go"
           You know, he held me close, I didn't let go.

Background: Jesus said "No! Don't let go" he held me close, I didn't let go.
Chorus: My Jesus loves me, so I can't let go (repeat 1 time)
Background: Loves me, so can't let go (repeat 1 time)

Verse 2:   I almost gave in; Satan tried to make me believe I couldn't win,
The terms of my salvation, brought about a situation.
Jesus said "No! Don't let go" You know, he held me close, I didn't let go.

Verse 3: Today is much the same, so much is coming against me, I don't know who to blame, when the load gets too heavy, Jesus comes to steady me.

Chorus 2: Still Jesus says "No! Don't let go" you know, he holds me close, so I don't let go.
My Jesus loves me, so I can't let go   (repeat 1 time)

Background: Jesus says "No! Don't let go" holds me close, so I don't let go.
Loves me so, can't let go   (repeat 1 time)

Addition to 2nd Chorus: You know, I'm here today, because of God's mercy
I'm here to say it's because of His amazing grace.
I hear Jesus saying "No! Don't let go" holds me close, so I don't let go.
Loves me so, can't let go.

THE LORD IS MY LIGHT AND MY SALVATION

Verse 1:

The Lord is my light and my salvation, whom shall I fear,
The Lord is the strength of my life, of whom shall I be afraid;
Though a host should encamp around me and the enemy comes against me,
In this will I be confident, for He is ever near.

Chorus:

The Lord is my shield, he provides my protection,
According to His commanding will,
There's no need for doubt, I'm assured he'll bring me out;
As in past times, he has done, and I praised Him for the victory won.

Verse 2:

Though trials comes with mass confusion, I will not be deterred,
I'm clothed with God's power, and faith abounding against the evil lure;
Having the helmet of salvation, the breastplate of righteousness,
The shield of faith, and the sword of the Holy Spirit.

MY FAITH LOOKS UP TO THEE, OH LAMB OF CALVARY

Verse 1:

My faith looks up to thee, oh Lamb of Calvary,
Glory; be thine, all the time.
I know you hear me every time I cry,
Even wipe my weeping eyes.
Stand near me, now I pray,
And strengthen me today.

Verse 2:

My faith looks up to thee, oh Lamb of Calvary,
Power is given to thee.
Protect me in the fight,
Hold me close with all your might.
Give me the victory over sin,
For Eternal Life to win.

Chorus:

Jesus, I stretch my hands to thee,
Oh Jesus, no one else can rescue me.
Jesus, you've been tried and found true,
Heaven's Gate awaits me, only you can guide me through.

LORD, I LOVE YOU MORE EACH DAY

Verse 1:

When I go to God in prayer, I do not have to worry,
For he always meet me there, sometimes in a hurry.
(Sing chorus)

Verse 2:

Sometimes, when evening comes and I feel things are wrong,
He comforts and He strengthens me, enlightens me through a song.
(Sing chorus)

Chorus:

You know, He makes my cloudy days so bright, He makes everything alright, that's why Lord, I love you more each day.

Verse 3:

When I'm in the heat of battle, I have no fear at all,
For I know He's with me, holding me firmly, lest I fall.
(Sing chorus)

Verse 4:

When enduring hardness as a soldier of the cross,
Sometimes I am tempted to ignore the gain, instead of loss.
(Sing chorus)

I'M COMING UP ON THE ROUGH SIDE OF THE MOUNTAIN

Verse 1:

I'm coming up on the rough side of the mountain,
Focusing on the Heavenly Prize, I won't turn back.
Empowered by our blessed fountain,
You know I'll never suffer lack.

Chorus:

I've got my helmet of salvation,
My sword is the Word of God.
Dressed in the breastplate of righteousness,
With the gospel my feet are shod.
Yes I'm coming up on the rough side of the mountain,
Hallelu, Hallelu, Hallelujah. (Repeat 1 time)

Verse 2:

I am determined, to do whatever it takes,
To reach the top, no matter what are the stakes.
Satan's attacks may slow me down,
But I will press my way, knowing I am homeward bound.

I WANT TO GO WHERE HEAVEN IS

Verse 1:

I want to go where Heaven is, be beneath the throne of God,
I want to go where Heaven is, transferred from this earthly sod.
With all my heart, never to depart from his presence!

Verse 2:

I want to be there in his arms, safe from all harm,
I want to join that Heavenly Choir, sing and never get tired.
Praising the Father and Jesus, His son for eternity!

Verse 3:

I want to be there when He's crowned King of Kings, and Lord of All,
I want to be in the midst of the Saints when my name is called.
Take my rest, among the blessed, to live forever more.

Chorus:

Hallelujah, Hallelujah, Hallelujah, Praise His Holy Name, Hallelujah,

Hallelujah, Hallelujah, Hallelujah, He's every day the same;

Hallelujah, Hallelujah, Hallelujah, to Jesus our King.

I JUST WANT TO SAY, THANK YOU LORD

Verse 1:

I just want to say thank you Lord,

Background: Thank you, thank you Lord,
                Thank you, thank you, thank you.

Background: Thank you, thank you Lord,
                You've been so good to me, opening doors which I could not see,
                And giving me the victory, over sin and then.

Verse 2:

I just have to say thank you Lord,

Background: Thank you, thank you Lord,
                Thank you, thank you, thank you;

Background: Thank you, thank you Lord,
                And if it took a million years, I could not tell in words exactly how I feel,
                All I can say, from day to day is thank you, thank you, thank you,
                Thank you Lord.

DRAW ME NEARER

Chorus: Draw me nearer, to thy bleeding side,
            Draw me nearer, where in you I can abide,
            Draw me nearer, nearer blessed Lord, to you.

VERSE # 1: Consecrate me now, as I humbly bow,
            With my heart opened up to thee;
            May I rise to the heights which I have not known,
            There forever to live beneath your throne.

VERSE # 1: Fortify me with your power divine,
            As I battle against this evil force, who would claim mine;
            Dedicated to your purpose Lord,
            Hand in hand with the Saints on one accord.

HOLD ON TO GOD'S HAND!

Verse #1: Life has a swift transition; you alone can not stand,
          Build your hopes on things eternal and hold on to God's hand.

Verse #2: When Satan comes to tempt you, just resist, don't be afraid,
          Speak the words Jesus commanded, and he will flee like Jesus said.

Verse #3: Time is short, it won't be long now, and Jesus is coming back again,
          Make your calling and election sure, be strong and true my friend.

Chorus: Hold on to God's hand, no matter what comes your way,
          Hold on to God's hand, whatever others do or say;
          Hold on to God's hand, and continue to pray,
          Victory will be yours at the break of day.

THE LOVE OF GOD

Verse # 1   The Love of God is greater than any words could ever tell,
             It reaches to the highest mountains and to the lowest vale.

Chorus: The Love of God, how rich, how pure, how measureless and strong,
             It will forevermore endure the Saints and Angels song.

Verse # 2:   The Love of God expels the notion that we are not to be as one,
             Salvation's plan gives us His favor through Jesus Christ, His son.

Verse # 3:   The Love of God is like no other, standing the test of time,
             It reaches to the highest mountains and to the lowest vale.

Verse # 4:   The Love of God is special but given to all mankind,
             Rejecting sin, accepting Jesus as Savior, will make Him say "you're mine".

PEACE LIKE A RIVER

Verse # 1: Peace like a river flows from God's hand,
Peace like a river is scattered throughout the land.

Verse # 2: Peace like a river is to be desired, not belittled,
Peace like a river akin to love can be rekindled.

Verse # 3: Peace like a river stirs my soul,
Peace like a river makes me glad I am whole.

Chorus: You know it flows throughout the mountains,
It flows throughout the valleys;
That peace like a river it flows inside of me,
(repeat chorus 1 time, then repeat; it flows . . .)

HARRY'S BIO

My name is Harry Wesley Youngblood Jr. born on August 14, 1965 in Chicago, Illinois to Harry and Aysha Youngblood. I am the oldest of their four children and number seven of the ten children by my mom.

I have a son (Tony) who will be 25 in December 2012 and a grand-daughter (Kinsley) who recently turned 1.

I served in the United States Army for 20 years in the Logistics field (76P and 92A) and I am now working in that same field as a civilian.

At present both of my parents live with me and God has blessed me to be able to abundantly care for my parents.

In the Promises of God, I Have Hope is the second book being published; the first one being (Put Some Honey on It). I had thought that I would have been came out with the second book before now, it's been 5 years between the two, but I find it peculiar how change of events took place recently to get to this point. I had written this poem titled "I Seen Love" and I recited it on the phone to a friend and I was telling her that once I write a poem for my Aunt Dorothy then I'll be ready to publish the second book. Two days later on March 23, 2012 while at work that morning, it had rained and started clearing up when I looked into the sky then picked up my pen and proceeded to write two poems. The first being "A Penny for Your Thoughts" and then "Matriarch . . . Thinking of You Aunt Dorothy" and things have just been falling into place ever since. Praise God! I'm elated and grateful!

PART 2:
HARRY'S SPIRITUAL RENDITIONS

A: SPIRITUAL POEMS

I SEEN LOVE

I seen love today, let me talk to you, please lend your ears,
I have been searching for love for most of a dozen years
And it has been right under my nose, matter of fact it continually reappears;
Images of her as I move past the fears and wipe away the tears!

You see love has a great wall,
Not focused on men, but of the angelic host and all.
Stories in the bible that applies to nowadays life she recall,
And love has uncommon faith that makes her stand tall.

Love is a word that few people really knows,
And the depth of it that it will make a lover goes.
Love notices everything about you from your hair to your toes,
Love expresses itself in deeds, letters, money, poetry, and prose.

Love will see you at your worst and fondly smile.
Love is old school with sayings like after while crocodile.
Love will come up with honey-do lists like laying down kitchen tile.
Love will prepare to go to the beauty parlor, kiss you and say I'll see you after awhile.

When two always desire to be in each other's company, that's love!
When two are joined as one, snug and cuddly, that's love that fits like a glove!
When its twenty years later and the fire is still there, that's a gift from above!
I see the characteristics, the mannerisms, the beauty, the brains,
and the essence of love.

CROSSROADS
NEEDMORE ROAD AND NEEDLESS ROAD

In to each life there will be rain,
Sometimes it's a blessing then again sometimes it's pain.

So I'm actively trying to find myself in spirituality, and in health,
In love, in family, and in a certain status of wealth!

One day I was looking out the window, leaning against the window sill,
And I had an unction to drive around this town that they call Clarksville.

So I'm driving down Wilma Rudolph Blvd and I make a right onto Needmore Road,
And it is here where the story begins to unfold.

For people always talk about what they need when it's actually wants that they desire,
Buying things that put their bank account in the red and their budget on fire.

But down this road I'm traveling, mainly because I'm intrigued by its name,
And I want to see if there is any significance, any history, or fame.

So Needmore Road I want to see what you are all about,
Are you some desolate road or do you have some clout.

And I found myself stopped at the corner of Needmore and Needless,
And I must confess that tunnel vision will leave you in a mess.

Somewhat like a thug that gets up in your chest and goes rat a tat tat,
Or foul situations like the rendition of Daddy's Little Girl by W.R.A.T.

So I'm at the corner and I'm thinking I need more,
But God is telling me that I need less.

And I say but God, you're a God of increase,
And he says yes, but your fleshly desires need to decrease.

Being less selfish is a part of it,
And getting more of the fruits of the Holy Spirit.

For in the flesh dwelleth no good thing,
And it's not about you, but it's all about the Kingdom, and what the Kingdom brings.

So here I am; free will leaves me at the crossroads with a critical decision,
And a wrong choice will lead to a painful transition.

But if I truly love God, I can travel that narrow road no matter how hard,
And I still would have visions of Miracle Boulevard.

ARISE TO LOVE

Wake up! Wake up!
Child of God, get up and do something, I implore you please,
We are in the heat of battle,
Pick up your sword or fall on your knees.

For freedom is not free
And neither is this Christian walk.
Our fore-fathers died blazing a path for us to follow
And our faith has to shine bright and back up our talk.

Holding forth the word of life,
So that our spirit can soar high and claim the prize
And we can be like the motto for United Airlines,
Flying the friendly skies!

So don't stay where you are,
But ascend to the Lord and he'll draw closer to you.
Trust him and never doubt,
And I guarantee you that there will be nothing that will be impossible for you to do.

Arise! With a doxology on your lips,
Arise! With meekness of heart,
Arise! To a Kingdom mindset, the Zoë kind of life,
Arise! To love and God's presence will not depart.

NOT TODAY

Birthdays are a time for celebration
And on August 14, 2008 my age increased in elevation,
And I thanked God for another year
But the following three nights God spoke in my ear.

Troubled my spirit and told me to go down stairs
And for two nights I did and went to sleep on the chaise lounge chair,
But that third night I was wide awake, and I sat on the couch trying to figure it out
Speaking to the Lord, Lord what is this all about?

And an hour after midnight, I seen the moon shine through the kitchen like never before,
Then a big and tall silhouette appeared at the threshold of that kitchen door,
And although I was naked as a jaybird, and in a vulnerable condition,
I growled and charged that position.

The intruder ran away,
And I praised God that day.
And a chant broke out, the devil is a liar, I could hear me say,
Along with not here! Not now! And not today!

MY SWAGGA

I'm getting my swagga back y'all and it'll be manifested, you'll see

Blessings are coming and over taking me,
I'm not just focused on myself and my family, but others in and out of the community.

I'm praying for my enemies as well
And I know that the accuser of the brethren, he wants me to fail,
But I just have to stay focused and realize that his destiny is set; he's got a one way ticket to hell.

Lord I pray that I stay humble and that my heart is true
And not to think highly of myself more than I ought to,
To continually seek guidance from you
And watch the marvelous things that you will do.

So I'm taking a stand today
That nowhere and no way,
Will I again give Satan room to have any kind of say.

That is going to impact my life,
Nor will I allow you to invade my spirit with strife,

For I'm drawing closer to the creator, and in doing so, I'm getting my swagga back.

TO GOD IN PRAYER # 2

Father God; I thank you for another day,
For allowing your precious gift to reside in me today,
Leading me along life's troublesome highway,
To speak life and not death in the words that I say;
Communing continually with you when I pray,
Lord establish the work of my hands each and every day,
And like the tree planted by the river, in your presence I want to stay,
For I shall be blessed from my rising to the time I hit the hay.

SERMON TITLES

Testing! Testing! Mic check one two one two, Mic check one two one two,
Preacher man! Yo preacher man, <u>can someone tell me what do you do
When life unravels?</u> When all hell breaks loose in your life,
When you feel like, you're number one, on the most wanted list of Satan's crew.

You know, <u>there's a thing going around town called willful sin,</u>
Where our young are lost in the streets, to drugs and domestic violence, being under scope,
Looking down the barrel of a shotgun
Trying to hold on to that last bit of hope.

And yes, there are skeletons buried in my past,
Lord knows that I have done my share of dirt,
Many acts I have long forgotten, but there are a few vivid memories
That if I think on them too long, it will still hurt.

The preacher tells me to walk upright before the Lord
And to be obedient in the sight of our creator,
Then to <u>just wait it out and watch God work it out,</u>
For Jesus Christ died on Calvary's cross, and our sins he bore.

I remember one day, I was watching the trees blow in the wind
And I heard the birds chirping, and I could hear a voice out of nowhere telling me,
<u>It's time for something new.</u>
<u>For you was born to taste the grapes</u> . . . you see!

Deeply absorbed in thought
I prayed for forgiveness and character,
And I asked the <u>Lord to strengthen me one more time.</u>
To <u>trust God through my seasons of waiting,</u> and my gift to stir!

And he put me on a new path, gave me a blueprint of my life
And instructions, sometimes singularly, sometimes in reps,
<u>Turning mistakes into miracles</u>
And <u>it's all by the grace of God, that he has ordered my steps.</u>

For no longer am I practicing a life of sin
For I gave my life to Christ and now I've been born again,
<u>Walking in the power of authority</u>
And <u>basking in the greatness of possibility,</u> I now see what God see's in me.

I thank God for this church, The Word of Life Ministries
And Pastor Mathis, for this is my emergency room, my filling station.
I've witnessed <u>the power of a praying church</u>
And I've learned a valuable bible lesson.

In the book of James it says to count it all joy
When you fall into diver's temptations,
Knowing that the trying of your faith worketh patience
And my faith has now taken on new heights and greater elevation.

Thank God for the gift of salvation and the power of his might,
Your assignment will always have an enemy, and you will be <u>beaten for the light.</u>
But just hang on in there, don't make any detours
Because saints and sinners are depending on you to stay in the fight!

And I heard Pastor Mathis asked a few questions, but I didn't hear a reply
When you answer them, you can be honest, there's no need to lie,
<u>Are you a jive turkey</u>? <u>Can you stand to be blessed</u>?
<u>Is your addiction greater than your faith</u>? Relax y'all there's no need to get stressed.

But I tell you this, the enemy is playing for keeps and he has turned up the heat,
The company that you keep will determine the trouble that you meet.
Make sure that your wants and desires
Don't handcuff you and land you in the lake of fire.

For <u>I can be up in a down world,</u>
The anointing caresses me, like the love of a woman, evolved from a girl
And for many, life is well
But don't lose focus of the bigger picture, because it is still holiness or hell.

Like that song that my mama wrote and sings with elegant grace,
I do it all for your glory, so that I can see your face.
You see, it's not about money or material things that I run this Christian race,
And I don't know why you do it, but <u>that's my story and I'm sticking to it</u>, I want to see his face.

The one who hung, bled, and died for me!
Who told me that I could be all that he created me to be!
From being a soldier in the army, to writing poetry, prose, and rhymes,
To the one who comforts me during the worst of times!

It hurts when loved ones pass on and when the tears cease to be at a steady flow,
I realize that both joy and sorrow helps me to grow.
I take comfort in knowing that the Word of Life fallen soldiers now have eternal victory, and we can all say,
I still have the power and presence of the Holy Trinity, I have you, and <u>I still got me.</u>

SAVE ME

Oh God! These are some terrible times
That we are living in,
The enemy has increased its attack, and dark days are filled with corruptible spirits
That is trying to depress me from within.

Haunting thoughts linger of cruel and unjust acts,
Sometimes I feel ready for you to take me Lord, but I'm not a quitter.
I have the intestinal fortitude to stand for truth,
It's just that these horrific tragedies make me bitter.

Lord, I want to be acceptable in your sight
And continue to show love to a dying world, that needs light.
Being humble, looking unto you and not my might,
To lead, guide, and strengthen me, for I know that this is right.

Saturate my mind, and give me your understanding and compassion,
Lord remember me,
Keep your hands upon me, and deliver me,
Lord please save me! . . . Save me!

I'M ON A DIET

I'm on a diet
And it's not to watch my calories or to live off of a variety of different vegetations,
But it is to cut the intake of negative conversations.

I'm on a diet
Not to control the size of my waist,
But to eliminate the abundance of gossip trying to invade my spirit, which is nothing but fatty waste.

So excuse me if I seem distant,
I don't mean to have you on ignore
But God is speaking, and I rather hear him more.

I don't want you upset with me, but I'm on a strict diet,
I have to make sure that there are no misunderstandings; I want to clear the air,
I'm living for the Kingdom of God now, and there are requirements to become an heir.

HE DRIED ALL OF MY TEARS

My tears, my tears, my tears,
He dried all of my tears.
All down through the years,
He gave me peace, whenever I was consumed with sorrow and fears.

But over twelve years ago, I was under an awful spell
Driving down I-24 from Cadiz, Kentucky to Fort Campbell;
Marriage and military careers seemingly on the rocks,
Like a bad episode from the show "Boondocks."

And I drove my Chevy Beretta off the highway into the median
Graveyard bound, and I can picture Satan salivating, beginning to grin.
Thinking that he can add to his list my name,
But God said not so as the paramedics came.

You know; Word of Life, without God I can truly say,
That I never would have made it to this present day;
My confidence, my hopes, my staying power
Would all be non-existent, spoiled and sour!

He brought me out of my dark seasons
And when I was lacking a desire to live, he gave me reasons.
Like a Ford, you're built tough;
Equipping me to stand when times get rough.

Soldier of the Lord rise to the top,
You are valuable, the cream of the crop.
Now take your place and walk in the light,
Witness to others and send demons to flight.

You're on the battlefield
And I've given you a sword and a shield.
Now stand up in the enemies face
And spread my love all over this place.

HOSPITALITY

H aving a clean heart,

O bserving and obeying God's word.

S erving the people of God and being spiritually discerning,

P utting away jealousy, lying, and back-biting for

I n this I tell you, corruptible spirits has no resting place in the life of a

T otally committed, Kingdom minded Christian. Who's

A lways willing to lend a helping hand,

L overs of life and being in His holy presence;

I t is we who give praise in spite of what today's situation might be.

T rouble don't last always, so give praise knowing that

Y our praise, your worship, and your tears is a down payment to your miracle.

BORN TO SERVE

From Genesis to Revelation,
There's knowledge to quench every temptation.

Everything I need was already put in place to get me over the learning curve,
I was born to serve.

I have to realize that this world doesn't revolve around me,
But my power, my peace, and my principles all comes from the Holy Trinity.

The Holy Spirit came to magnify the light,
So let every man be a liar, because serving God is right.

Like Dirty Harry, I'm locked and loaded, and ready to fight,
Spitting lyrics from these 66 books and praying throughout the night.

Greeters, door keepers, armor bearers, and praise and worshippers,
Nursery workers and kitchen committee workers don't take your position lightly.

You have to be spirit filled, prayed up, and on your post,
For the enemy is continually seeking, planning, and attacking nightly.

Lift up in prayer and support the angel of this church,
Ask the Lord to purify whatever he finds unclean in his search.

God is a God of decency and order, and a respecter of authority,
So hospitality, hygiene, obedience, and a prayer warrior must be your priority.

Whatever you put your hands to do, or where ever your feet may trod,
It's how you treat other people that reflect your relationship with God.

It's not what you eat or drink that defiles a man, but what comes out of the mouth,
And many saints are talking themselves into a first class ticket to the Deep South.

Living a hellacious life but on Sunday displaying a Godly form,
Your reward will be weeping and gnashing of teeth in an eternal fiery storm.

Jesus Christ is our example
And all throughout scripture through parables and deeds, he gave us a sample.

Heal the sick, open blinded eyes, these things and greater shall you do in my name,
For when you become His partner, your life will never again be the same.

A question came; can your faith affect people like Michael Jackson's cd thriller?
Are your prayers effective demon killers?

There is honor in serving God, be determined like Joshua did with a resounding chord,
As for me and my house, we're going to serve the Lord.

For a man is justified by works and not by faith alone,
My name is victory and there is life in these dry bones.

You have got to establish an atmosphere for a miracle,
That's 360 degrees of praise, prayer, faith, wisdom, and courage to complete the circle.

So I'm going to launch out into the deep, oh yes! I have the nerve,
For I know that God's anointing rest on me and I was born to serve.

LORD, I THANK YOU FOR MY LIFE
(For Evangelist Ella Preston)

Before the beginning of time
You had me in mind,
You provided everything I would ever need
But in faith the mysteries of life I would find.

And looking back from being a little girl in Toledo, Ohio
And now being a woman in Clarksville, Tennessee.
You have been my rock, my Lord, and my redeemer,
Your hand has continually been upon me.

Sometimes my life has been seemingly going in circles
Like a child playing with a hoola hoop,
But if I just stand still and seek your face,
You'll lead me to a righteous path out of the loop.

Lord, I thank you for my life!
And the godly man that affectionately calls me his wife.
In marriage together we have this ministry,
And we owe it all to thee.

You have touched my hands
To play skillfully,
You anointed my voice
For me to sing praises of your glory.

And because you love me like that,
I'll forever give you the praise.
Because you love me like that,
The talents you've blessed me with, I'll tithe all of my days.

Lord, I thank you for all that you have done,
The ups and downs, the joys and sorrows,
For giving me another tomorrow
And with your mercy and grace, I'll continue to grow.

Lord, I thank you!
Lord, I thank you for my life!

WHISPERS IN THE DARK

Whispers in the dark
Each with its own definitive voice,
Assaulting my eardrums
With distinct familiar sounds;
Riding the winds of eternity
Ushering in words of wisdom,
Fear, pain, caution, and love;
So many whispers,
All calling my name
Speaking crystal clear,
Lingering, hounding, haunting.
Seeking a response,
Nudging me in the side,
Invading my psyche
Causing sleep deprivation;
Hellish nightmares
And vexing my soul,
Provokingly
As I recognize these voices
That now speaks in the wind,
Those of ex lovers
And past significant others;
Seeking riddance
Summoning Greek legends,
Morpheus and Orpheus
To extricate them,

But this is preposterous
As I get a grip,
Waking up in a cold sweat
Putting things in perspective,
I kneel down and pray
Calling on the Father
The creator of everything,
And the whispers in the dark immediately fade away.

THE THRILL IS GONE

Dear Satan:

The bible states that man born of woman is but of a few days and full of trouble,
And through sin it's your intentions to leave us in ruin and rubble.
And for part of my life I danced with the devil and you influenced my will,
But everything was temporal, enticing me with various pleasurable thrills.

And contrary to popular belief, sin does feel really good at times,
But on the flip side, against God it's a serious crime.
Not to mention that it creates a chain reaction of situations,
That'll disturb my peaceful abode and in distress demand I take an action.

And somewhat like a Dear John letter I'm here to inform you,
That the thrill is gone and I'm exiting the door, we're through.
Yes, you're right a certain type of woman can move me,
But I'll be alright as long as my focus is on the Holy Trinity.

And I've learned from experience that what looks good to me
Isn't necessarily good for me,
And not to make someone a priority and give all my attention,
When all that they do is view me as an option.

Satan, I have to thank you for your shallow promises,
And I really can appreciate now the things that Jesus says.
For I find that he wants to bless and empower me,
Here now on earth and throughout all eternity.

While you're going on and on with idle chatter,
You're just a scam artist trying to hoodwink me, him, and her.
Masking your motives and tactics with a chess pawn,
But I pray that others will come to realize the truth and serve notice to you that the thrill is gone.

JEHOVAH IS A ROCK; I'M A WITNESS

Jehovah is an awesome God,
Looking over his creation with each step that we may trod.
Providing a way for us to address him directly in a particular need,
And each of his names releases into our lives a different seed.

And no matter what denomination or category you may classify yourself to be,
You can be a Christian, Jehovah Witness, Catholic, Muslim, Baptist, or A.M.E.
But when you speak in faith, you will unleash in your life God's power,
Like praying for the sick, we lift up Jehovah Rapha, the Lord our healer at that particular hour.

At times your way may be foggy, or your spirit may be a little blue,
But we can look to Baal-perazim, the God of a break through.
Dialing up the Lord our provider, that's Jehovah Jireh,
And not forsaking or leaving us, for Yahweh is present and EL ROI always looks upon His son and daughter.

The enemy tends to attack those who try to live Godly the most,
But the antidote is of course Jehovah Shabaoth, the Lord of Host.
And to those that love God, He's not hid,
Jehovah is a rock; I'm a witness and He is solid.

PASTOR MILLER
Sulphur Springs A.M.E. Pastoral Anniversary 10/5/2008

Pastor Menjou Miller is a very energetic and approachable man of God,
He has the people skills to reason with another without dominating the conversation.
Revered by many and loved by all,
He lives by example of building on a solid foundation.

We've all had our time as a babe in Christ,
But Pastor Miller is a man that is making a career out of this Christian Ministry.
Upholding the great commandment and the great commission,
Just take a listen to him as he share golden nuggets to bless the life of you and me.

And I can hear the word say in Psalms 1:1
Blessed is he that walk not in the counsel of the ungodly,
But his delight is in the word of God,
With a promise that he shall live in prosperity.

I heard somewhere before that your spouse is a reflection of what God thinks of you,
And if that is so, then God's favor rest upon him in this walk of fame.
Because he has a woman that is God-fearing and also capable of being his backbone,
She is submissive to him but not afraid to address him by name.

You see as you honor him, you should honor both,
Because joined at the hip they are one.
20 plus years in marriage and ministry,
Having peaks and valleys throughout, but won't quit until God says it's done.

Being a preacher, pastor, or first lady, we know is not an easy task,
Having counseling sessions, sometimes needing to pray way before you attempt to talk.
Listening to our complaints and our doubts,
While at the same time trying to teach and guide us in this spiritual walk.

We bless God for the angel of this church,
Preaching and teaching Jesus, creating an atmosphere for the Holy Spirit to fall.
Knowing that only what you do for Christ will last, so open your heart,
And be receptive of the Spirit as the Pastor concludes with an alter call.

I DO IT ALL FOR YOUR GLORY

I do it all for your glory
And if I get to testify, I'll tell my story,
Of how you came into my life and your countenance glowed upon my face.
And the life that I live displays a body of work and not just a trace.

I'm dwelling in the secret place of God in all of His glory,
And it causes me to abide under the shadow of the Almighty.
I dare to share God's gifts,
And I can't count the numerous times that my spirit He did lift.

It is because of the God in me,
That I'm kind to those that are bad apples, fallen from a tree.
Trying to let my light shine bright,
As I rely on the Lord to strengthen me and not my might.

Being mindful of the price that you paid for me,
Way back on that old rugged cross at Calvary.
How on the cross you said that it was finished,
And you're steadily encouraging me that my purpose and my value, to let no man diminish.

I'm a soldier praying for the saints, sinners, and my family,
I'm a humble servant living to give you the praise and all the glory.

DEACON JOHNNIE WHITE

D eacon Johnnie White
E nabling others
A lways a voice of reason
C aring for others
O bserving to keep the unity
N avigating matrimony well

J oined at the hip for 30 plus years in marriage
O bserving the precious jewel that he found in her
H earkening her every desire
N ever taking her for granted
N or the nuptials
I nducing
E verlasting endearment

W hen heaven called
H aving been found to be a man of character
I ntegrity now speaks
T here is meaning for my life
E xiting this world being purposefully positioned

FRAME THAT PICTURE

Well it's another year
And my love is forever with you dear,
I keep you close to my heart
And the bond we share guarantees your memory won't depart.
I tell you, there's nothing like family,
And your smile I continually long to see;
I picture us shopping, playing cards, or you calling my name,
And all those precious memories I've encased in a loving frame.
I just want to take a little time out of my busy day,
Reflecting and rejoicing with you today.
And no matter what the occasion is i.e. anniversary, holiday, or birthday,
I always think of you and then I begin to pray.

Happy Birthday Kerri!
September 2009

LEGACY

What is the legacy that you want to leave behind?
What kind of history will your grandchildren find?

Will it be one of a menace to society?
Will it be one of tears and shame for a dynasty?

Will it be one that says that you were part of the solution?
Instead of part of the problem or will it be a fusion of a chaotic proportion?

Will your life be the example for your children to follow?
Or will it be void of a prayer life, rendering it hollow?

A nation running amuck, a culture so cold and icy,
A race that is out for itself, for your part, what is your legacy?

REMEMBERING KATRINA

Vivid memories of that fateful day,
When Katrina rocked Louisiana and a couple more states;
Leaving a trail of destruction in her wake, altering lives forever.
You see that picture up above; it was taken a year ago,
With the trauma still fresh, I wept.
I cried for my family, my loved ones, my city, and my state,
For many was swept away in the torrential rains;
Corpses floating in the city streets, diseases were spreading everywhere.
Our government provided little help and there was so much anger that I harbored,
Once I realized that the government and the president were neglecting our needs.
I guess it is because we're not well off, or in the in-crowd,
You see aid came quickly to Texas, why is that? Was it because that's his home state?
I digress
Well it's been a year now and this government is still throwing salt into open wounds,
More concerned about oil and politics than humanity.
What's up with the levees? You've been playing tag for 12 long months now,
And with another hurricane season upon us, I'm feeling a lot of things.
Mad, angry, concerned, and prayerful to name a few,
And with all of this in my view, not wanting to be homeless again,
I remember, contemplate, pray, and shed a few more tears.

ATTITUDES

A person's attitude sometimes draws people and it can also push them away,
Why do people keep walking out of your life? Why won't they stay?
I'm not naïve, in a human's life periodically a bad one will come and go,
But your spirit of love should be dominant and for the most part it should show.

You can't display the badge of being a child of God among the crowd,
Then turn around behind closed doors and do innuendos or criticize people aloud.
Conjuring up in your mind that it's displaying righteous indignation,
When in all actuality it's just gossiping and creating a bad situation.

By loving kindness have I drawn you?
That's what Jesus said and that's what we should do.
We as children of God is not in the business of harassment nor belittlement,
We are to show love, speak in faith and with our fellow man come into agreement.

You shouldn't be the cause of making anyone dread coming to the House of Prayer,
Your attributes, demeanor, and actions should all indicate that you care.
Lord, I pray that you touch each and every heart,
That these relationships will bond together instead of severing apart.

Convict us Lord where we are wrong,
And in the mending process give us a joyful song.
I declare that my attitude is one of love, peace, and harmony,
Desiring to live and worship in the spirit of unity.

ECHOES IN THE WIND

Echoes in the wind
Resonate and send
The voice of my friend

My heart is heavy,
And the tears are flowing steadily.
How can I keep this home from becoming just a house?
While I'm in the grieving process of losing my spouse!
How can I look for the rainbow?
When I'm in the midst of so much sorrow,
The future is now ever before me,
How can I push past the pain and accept the challenge to still effectively raise our family?

Echoes in the wind
Resonate and send
The voice of my friend

We was just talking about two hours ago and I was gleaming from every word that you said,
My heart! My love! I can't believe that you're now dead.
I feel cheated out of our lifetime together,
And I can't even name all the emotions within me that are beginning to stir.
My daughters need their mother,
And no matter how hard I try to provide and teach, I could never have the impact of her.
For a mother's love has a way of making everything alright,

It encourages you to continue to press on and to take flight.
Lord; my life and that of my children, you know it's intention,
And I'm crying out to you for divine intervention.
Move by your spirit into the affairs of my life,
Cast away all confusion and strife.
God you speak and the earth will respond,
You called my name and now I'm no longer a vagabond.
You changed my life and in righteousness I want to live to the end,
But right now I really need to hear from my friend.
I know that now she is one with you,
And when I speak with you, I'm also speaking with her too.
I never had the chance to say a proper goodbye and I just wanted you to know,
That no matter where I may go, my love for you will continue to show.

Echoes in the wind
Resonate and send
The voice of my friend

REAL TALK

They tell me that what comes from the heart reaches the heart,
And there is a lot going on in my mind right now that I don't really know where to start.
I don't think that I'm better than anyone else, I'm just a sinner saved by grace,
And with any new relationship with meaning, you put extra effort into cleaning your place.
And so it is now that Jesus has come into my life,
I'm more keenly alert of what is required to join that collective body that will become His wife.
The more that I understand the laws of God and the workings of the Holy Trinity,
It causes me to see myself in the true light and that I am so unworthy.
And I know that it disappoints God when I slip and fall,
And it makes it all the more so amazing; that my name He still call!
Using everything as a teachable moment and always displaying genuine love,
My child; don't continue to wallow in the mud, but pick yourself up and ascend up above.
For destiny is waiting on you,
But you have to follow the instructions that I have given you to do.
I have placed an anointing on your life and have given you talents and gifts,
And I'm asking you to stay focused on me so that your mind won't drift.
Don't get caught up in the lights and the glamour,
For the enemy is lurking; seeking to deliver a blow to you with a spiritual sledge hammer.
But be strong in the grace that is in Christ Jesus,
And no demonic force will be able to devour you or to separate us.

I MISS YOU

I knew you before there was an earth,
I saw your strengths, your weaknesses, and I know your worth.

Over 2000 years ago,
My father told me to go.

I paid a debt that I didn't owe,
Displaying my love, being patient, and giving you room to grow.

I long for us to be close,
You and I to be tighter than most;

To be like that three strand cord,
But with me you are acting bored.

We're supposed to be road dawgs,
But somehow you got lost in the fog.

Being seduced by money, flattery words, and sexy sights,
Having you captivated, going on rendezvous late into the night.

You say that you love me but you won't spend any time with me in your house,
You make me feel like I'm married to a very neglecting spouse.

Quick to criticize people calling them a hypocrite,
But how in the world do you think that you're legit.

I see you and my heart grieves,
Do you really think that it's hidden from the heavenlies?

Let me tell you child of God, a hidden secret on earth,
Is just an open scandal in heaven, and not the seed that you want birthed.

How long shall I suffer you?
What will it take to get you to walk by my word and stay true?

It's time out for straddling the fence,
Your decisions will determine the consequence.

And as you get ready to cross over into 2009,
Know this! It's all or nothing, now is the time.

Get right church!
And let's go home!
I Miss You!

THESE HANDS THAT I HOLD

Into each life defining moments will come,

Some very profound accompanied by revelation and wisdom.

As I sat down to eat and talk with my friend,

We went into prayer holding hands which is our trend.

Father God! Thank you for these hands that I hold,

For the lady that oozes with femininity, spirituality, and a heart of gold.

Thank you for the many aspects of this fellowship,

Birthing a firm foundation upon which we built this relationship.

Centered in the word of God,

Giving respect to our Lord and to ourselves as we navigate life upon this earthly sod.

A woman that works hard and gives so much of herself,

Serving the people of God, but sometimes I'm concerned about her health

But in times when she is sick and in times when she purr,

I made up in my mind that I'm going to serve her.

Much like Jesus said that he came not to be served but to serve,

And I'm following his example as I get through this learning curve.

I'm going to carry myself like a husband until I become one indeed,

And I will not plant any superficial seeds.

Nor will I erroneously say something that I don't mean,

My word will be my bond, something you can rely on and lean.

For that is what a husband does,

Forever mindful of his spouse and doing things for her out the blue just because;

And I'm reminded that a man that finds a wife, he finds a good thing and baby you're a pot of gold,

You are very dear to my heart and it's my desire that as we grow old, it's your delicate hands that I hold.

IN THE PROMISES OF GOD, I HAVE HOPE

I PETER 5:10 KJV
But the God of all grace, who hath called us unto his eternal glory by Christ Jesus, after that ye have suffered a while, make you perfect, stablish, strengthen, settle you.

It is in the valley that our lives experience various dangers
And we sometimes call on special operation forces like the elite rangers,
To come and find and rescue,
To do what they have been trained to do.

But I know a man that is a present help in the time of trouble
And he loves to continually bust the enemies bubble.
He sends his angelic host to wage war for me
And to pronounce victory, healing, and prosperity,

For in our sufferings miracles are birthed
And through our character and God's grace we'll know our worth.
And after awhile . . . . that unknown period of time,
I'll get rid of the stench of the suffering and of the grime.
To once again live the abundant life,

Like Job did after his ordeal, and received double for his trouble, and quieted his wife.
The sky is the limit when you have a solid relationship with the Father
And you'll be purposefully positioned to testify of the goodness of God to another.

So I have hope in God's promises, like after the rain I look for a rainbow,
And I establish an atmosphere each day to let the Holy Spirit in my life, get on the go.
So I speak his word and on that word I do stand,
For every promise of God is yea and amen.

B: TRIBUTE POEMS

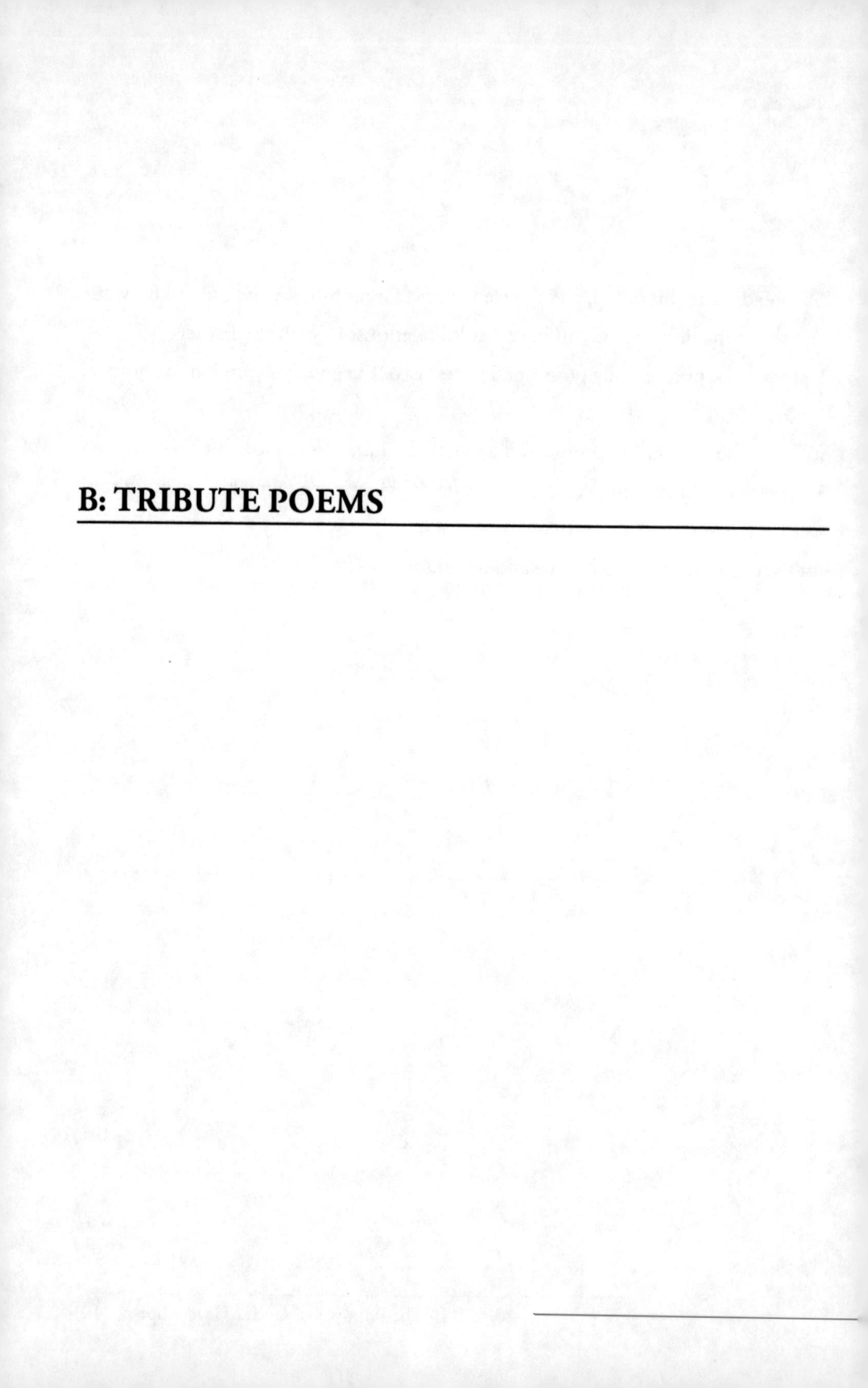

from left to right: Martha, Sam, Dorothy, Harry, and Barbara (Youngblood siblings)

MATRIARCH .... THINKING OF YOU AUNT DOROTHY

As I look out the window and into the sky, I see a pretty blue hue
And I'm already thinking of you,
The love and compassion you displayed
And I have to believe that on numerous occasions for me, you prayed.

And I'm a witness that God answers prayer
And I'm excited to think that with him, you're there.
Chillin with the heavenly host
And I seal that in my thoughts to comfort me, while our conversations I miss the most.

Aunt Dorothy I just wanted to let you know,
That your brother has his prosthetic leg now and in therapy he's on the go.
Doing more than what is required of him,
Putting a positive spin on a situation that once was grim;

I remember you calling me when you couldn't get him on the phone
And I sensed the despair in your voice that he might be hurt and alone.
And when I found him in the hospital and called so that you all could talk,
He was lying down in bed with a severe leg wound, but I had a vision that he could walk.

And his conversation to you was that he's not lost anymore, because Jr. found me
And as the two of you talked, I could tell that he held on to his sister's love tightly.
And six months later you went to be with the Lord on a first class flight,
And when I told him, all he said was that you put up a good fight.

To Larry and Denise, you was the matriarch to your family,
As well as to your grandchildren, friends, and the community,
And I remember at your home going ceremony, your memory dried all of our tears,
And gave us something to hold onto for the rest of our years;

Show love to this dying world, you can accomplish anything you set your mind to do,
You are kingdom men and women; God's favor is upon you,
And as I gaze into that beautiful blue sky above,
Your memory warms my heart and I cherish the love.

A love that will never die

CHERISH THE LOVE

This is a letter to my sons, John and James!
And as your father will say every now and then,
You are the sons of thunder
But to me, you are my special young men.
You are the very best of your father and I,
And we have instilled in you the essence of love.
Love that transcends time,
Love that is the trinity, the God-head above;
When you love somebody so very deeply, it's extremely hard to let go.
So it's ok to shed tears, and right now they are tears of sorrow,
But I promise you one day, they will turn to tears of joy,
And fond memories of me will fill your tomorrow.
My time on earth has ended
But I'll never cease to live,
For in the hearts of my children,

My love will continue to give.
With every fiber in my body
I loved you the most,
And I'll be your guardian angel
Up there with the heavenly host;

Life here, where I am is so wonderful,
A beautiful place that just yet you cannot see;
Walking the golden shores,
Just my Savior and me!
I wish that you could see me now,
I'm whole again, no sickness and no pain.
I've accepted Jesus in my life
And now I have obtained eternal gain.
John; I've heard that a good man does not make his wife jealous,
But he makes other women jealous of her.
And the plans that you and Jamilla had planned,
It truly touched my heart, you have my blessings, and she's a keeper.
And James; don't ever change who you are,
Continue to stay loving and affectionate,
Keep your trust in God,
And your fire will always stay lit.
I'm so Godly proud of the both of you,
Your goals and your dreams continue to seek to do.
For you are mighty men of God
I'll be with you in spirit, so don't feel blue, and know that I truly do love you!

Dedicated to the memory of Wanda Jo Mathis
A mighty woman of God

A PENNY FOR YOUR THOUGHTS

Gazing off into the sunset,
I recall to remembrance this wonderful lady that I met.
One who's smile lit up the place
And in our hearts occupied a permanent space,
The warmth of her love radiated
And many were fixated
As well as elated
That God took extra care in this woman that he created.
His blessing was upon her
And evident even through a picture,
In her was so much joy
Largely due to her girl (Phyllis) and her boy (Robert);
For a parent their children becomes the apple of their eye
And sometimes they laugh, and sometimes they cry.
I remember in the hospital, the peace she displayed as I sang her God's song
And the fellowship that followed when her family came along.

I can imagine her doing the super bowl shuffle
Chanting Da Bears! All the way, or dancing to the Chicago slide or to the hustle.
Full of life and an audience she's always caught
So on this day, I give you a "penny" (Henrietta Adams) for your thoughts,
Safe in the master's arms, there is no need for alarm, no need to call the police
For truly she is resting in peace!

Cherished Memories

ON THE WINGS OF LOVE

There are many things in this life
That we can't understand,
But if we trust in our creator
He promises safe passage by holding on to his hand.
I have to be honest that it grieves me to leave you like this
And all of you I will sorely miss.
Last night I cried a river, to keep my family strong and together,
Seeking divine provision from this stormy weather,
But I won't complain and neither should you,
I'm grateful for the time that we've had to share.
And the joys and sorrows that we went through,
We've had our share of ups and downs, but in love, as a family, we do care.

Mama, I can't even begin to comprehend your pain
But I do know that the rainbow comes after the rain,
And like the morning dew
Let God's comforting spirit rest upon you.

Aysha M. Youngblood-Moses & Harry W. Youngblood Jr.

I am my mother's daughter
And I come from a long line of gorgeous and strong-minded women.
From Leila, Easter, and Pearlean
To Shandra, Harvetta, Charlotte, Diane, Pat, and Sherika
And we are sho-nuf a piece of work (smiling).
Mama, do you remember Shandra playing Gladys Knight
And me, Harvetta, and Charlotte being the Pips
Performing Midnight Train to Georgia,
Hmmm . . . maybe Charlotte should have raised a collection for tips
Because we didn't get paid like they did, but we had so much fun
And that's one memory that I'll always cherish.

To my fiancé David
You have been heaven sent since you came into my life,
The love and friendship is awesome, ten wonderful years together
And I'm excited to become your wife.

To my children
Ritchie, Vanera, Clifford Jr.
Willie, Justina, and Kyeisha
A mother's love is unconditional
And loving you has been my greatest accomplishment.
My love will never die,
I'm flying on the wings of love
Having joined that cloud of witnesses,

And I'll be your guardian angel
To help you through life's troublesome way;
Always believe in yourself and dream big dreams,
Speak positive about your life and positive things will happen.
There's so much that I want to say
But sometimes words get in the way,
So I'll just close with this, if you need me just call;
During the day, or after nightfall
And no matter how hard your day may seem,
Just call me and I'll meet you in your dreams.

Love and Kisses
Kerri

But above all . . . Jesus is love
And I'm resting on those wings now

A SAINT'S GRADUATION DAY

Every time I turn around God is blessing me.
From Jacksonville beaches to heaven's glorious shores,
Favor has been upon me,
And opened up many doors;

God loves me like crazy, how awesome is that?
That my birth and home-going celebrations would be on the same day but 18 years apart,
How awesome is that? He blessed me with a standing room only send off and
A heavenly mansion has been prepared for me, because of my heart.

To Phillip and Harvetta Jackson; my loving parents,
Your sacrifices and tough love, I appreciate more than I can ever say;
And though the outcome wasn't as you pictured it, you made me a better man,
A better father, a better child of God; preparing me for my graduation day.

Psalms 116:15 says "precious in the sight of the Lord is the death of his saints"
So celebrate my life, that is my wish for you and Sean my son,
And no matter what the physical evidence is
Just know that in Christ, the victory has already been won.

I'm a beast on the field, always full steam ahead; I won't yield until the battle is won.
Victory! Oh what a sweet smelling aroma,
I'm going to get hyped and do my dance to the Lambo, and sing many a song,
All the while celebrating my spiritual diploma;

Matter of fact, I'm going to sit at the master's feet,
Review my life and he's going to tell me what it's all about.
My spirit shall never die; I'm a saint, from Sandalwood High to New Covenant Ministries, I'm a saint,
I'm a saint for life! I'm at peace, and I'll see you on higher ground, number 6 out.

There is laid up for me the crown of righteousness, which the Lord,
the righteous judge shall give me at that day.

IN THE MASTER'S HAND

Wow! The whole atmosphere here is just so grand,
And I am safe in the master's hand.
Having moved from labor to reward,
But I'll never stop praising my God, my Savior, and my Lord.
For He has been so very good to me,
He empowers me to continually walk in a posture of victory.
And I'm not ignorant to the enemy's devices,
So I'm always alert and ready to speak what God says.
For in God's word there is liberty and freedom,
And I'm continually ministering to God's people . . . the saint, the sinner, and the bum.
And I know that the enemy is watching me here and there,
So I'm quick to swing my belt, giving a whipping to the prince of the air.
And as I draw closer to the twilight of my years,
I'm looking more and more to see my Jesus, I have no fears.
Lynn and Darrise; don't buy no more food for me,
For in glory soon I will be.

Don't you forget what I taught you down through the years!
And watch the manifestation of God's promises be real in your life my dear.
Don't you worry about me for I am safe in the master's hand!
Worshipping my God; with the heavenly band.
I am free, praise the Lord I'm free, no longer bound, no more chains holding me,
My soul is resting, and it's such a blessing, praise the Lord, Hallelujah I'm free.

God's Battle Tested Angel

Mrs. Olivia Smith

Aunt Libby

PURPOSEFULLY POSITIONED

As my mind reflect back,
I'm reminded of a Word of Life soldier that was on the right track.
Traveling down that narrow road to glory,
And at times he would share part of his story.
Of just how good God has been to him,
And how over the years his faith had put on weight, no longer is it puny and slim
A man determined to live this faith lifestyle,
Teaching his children to be constant in the things of God, and not every once in awhile.
How at the men's prayer breakfast, he was cooking bacon, eggs, and all,
And once he wrote a letter to the deacons in the fashion of the Apostle Paul.
And I believe that it blessed lives that day,
Touching the hearts of some to be reenergized and continue on in the way.
Before he passed he was working on a sermon titled "Purposefully Positioned"

A powerful title that many will not forget and in their hearts it'll stay conditioned.
I can picture Deacon Johnnie White on the first pew,
Standing on his feet as the praises of God swept through.
Putting his hand on his ear; tuning up his vocal chords,
Not being ashamed to praise the Lord.
Singing a song of a life in Christ that didn't roam,
I'm going to put on my robe and tell the story of how I made it over, soon as I get home.

C: BONUS SECTION- POEMS AND CORRESPONDING SERMON NOTES

1. Who Can I Trust
2. You Can Trust In God
3. The Life of a Soldier
4. A Soldier Story; The Life of a Soldier-Dealing with Adversity

WHO CAN I TRUST?

Mama's baby, Daddy's maybe,
There's so much drama in this world today that it sometimes leaves you disgusted
And at one time a mother was someone that you could almost always depend on,
But nowadays even mama can't be trusted.

When parents, pastors, parishioners, mentors, and siblings
Become role models best suited for the state penitentiary.
And high society forecast doesn't look to get any brighter,
Then who can I trust? What kind of hope does that leaves me?

Thank God that people isn't my only option,
And I also realize that I'm not wise enough to handle everything by myself.
I need something concrete, a divine intervention,
So I pray to Jehovah, for in Him is my hope, my trust, my peace, and also my source of wealth.

YOU CAN TRUST IN GOD

PSALMS 71: 1-9   7/2011

Many of us at one time or another has put our trust in a man, or in a woman, in family, and in friends, only to be let down and disappointed when things didn't happen the way that you expected them to.

Sometimes disappointments, tests, trials, and sorrows can weigh you down so bad to the point where you hit rock bottom and you feel that you are all alone. It is at rock bottom where your pride and stubbornness leaves you and God can get your attention, and it is at rock bottom where the foundation of the Lord is laid, for Jesus said upon this rock I will build my church and the gates of hell shall not prevail against it.

Sometimes as a child of God, your lack of trust in people will cause you to distant yourself and in essence become sort of a recluse and you find yourself not wanting to be around people.

Not even wanting to come to the House of Prayer!

We as humans are faulty people,

Sometimes we let people down,

Sometimes we let our own self down.

And we find ourselves asking the question,

Who can I trust?

And today I want to share a couple of minutes with you

Just to say

You can trust in God!

The bible says in Psalms 71 beginning with the first verse (read 1-9)

You can trust in God for peace, protection, and provision.

You can trust in God for love, liberty, and life.

You can trust in God for faithfulness, food, and to not to forsake us in our old age.

God cares about every detail of your life;

He collects every tear in a bottle . . .   Psalms 56:8

He numbers every hair on your head . . .   Luke 12:7

He knows every hurt in your heart . . .   Psalms 34:18

He knows every enemy that comes against you . . .   Psalms 3:1

Many are the afflictions of the righteous;

But the Lord delivers him out of all of them.

So give all your cares and all your concerns to God,

Because he cares for you . . . 1 Peter 5:7

God says as a mother comforts her child,

So will I comfort you . . . Isaiah 66:13

Psalms 71: 17-18 says "Oh God, thou hast taught me from my youth: and hitherto have I declared thy wondrous works

Now also when I am old and grey-headed,
O God forsake me not; until I have showed thy strength unto this generation
And thy power to everyone that is to come!

I thank God for you,

Your life is a testimony.

I think to my Aunt Libby

Mrs. Olivia Smith, 92 years of age,

That is now in a nursing home in Illinois,

A minister in her own right,

Who is now bed-ridden, but has a niece that regularly goes to see her and tend to her needs

Her whole life has been and still is centered on Jesus,

Praising God is truly what she does.
And I think back to David

When he penned the verses that says

I once was young and now I'm old

And I never seen the righteous forsaken,

Nor its seed begging bread;

I hear Paul say that he that began a good work in you

Shall perform it until the day of Jesus Christ;

So I tell you today, put your trust in God!

Get centered in his will, which is the word of God.

Matter of fact bible experts has the center of the bible as Psalms 118

Some say verse 8, while others say verses 8 and 9

And it reminds us to trust in God

Over trusting in ourselves or other people

God has so much that he wants to do in your life,

But you have got to invite him in to your heart

Build a relationship with God.

For with God nothing shall be impossible unto you,

He has placed a treasure in you

And you have got to respect that treasure, and honor it.

God is looking for diamonds in the rough,

People that will launch out into the deep

And stand on his every word, in spite of adversity

In spite of situations that arises in our lives

Knowing that those who love the Lord

Are often persecuted

But realize this

That your trust in God

Does not get you around trouble, but it gets you through it.

God is a sustainer!

Praise the Lord for he is glorious!

Never shall his promise fail!

God has made the saints victorious;

Sin and death shall not prevail,

Praise the God of our salvation!

Host on high, his power proclaim;

Heaven and Earth, and all creation,

Magnify his holy name.

Put your trust in God

And everything will be alright.

God Bless You!

THE LIFE OF A SOLDIER

The life of a soldier is not an easy life,
Some soldiers wear more than one hat.
Being a husband, wife, or single parent,
Not to mention being trained and training others for military and or spiritual combat.

The life of a soldier is full of demands and challenges,
And on any given day there can be many twists and turns
With physical and mental tests,
That sometimes the best of them on occasion emotionally crash and burn.

But it is through the testing times that we develop and get stronger,
It is through adversity that you see who or what a person leans on.
And with determination and hope we learn to hang on just a little while longer.
And for some you can actually see their faith being born.

A soldier of faith!
A soldier believes that victory is in their future
And though he or she may sweat, shed tears, or even bleed,
The finish line is clear because in their minds they painted a meticulous picture.

A SOLDIER STORY; THE LIFE OF A SOLDIER- DEALING WITH ADVERSITY 2/2012

It is my belief that the things that we go through in this life, is not only to strengthen us, not only to be a lesson to us, but also we go through situations in this life to be able to help someone else down the line.

And it is in this context that I will be coming from a theme of A Soldier Story/The Life of a Soldier-Dealing with Adversity. I would like to invite your attention to two passages of scripture

2 Timothy 2:3 "Thou therefore endure hardness, as a good soldier of Jesus Christ"

And also Psalms 3 in its entirety

Psalms 3 "a Psalm of David when he was on the run from his own son Absalom"

Here we have Paul and David; two mighty men of God, who at times in their life faced and overcame adversity. Who at times in their life; had to encourage themselves in the Lord. They were soldiers, who were all about accomplishing the mission; which is to please God.

For it is recorded that David was a man after God's own heart, and Paul gave maximum effort to whatever he was doing, when his name was Saul and he was persecuting the saints, he gave it all that he had, and when his name was changed to Paul and he started lifting up the Kingdom of God, he gave it all that he had.

It is amazing to me how God orchestrates the events and the affairs in your life, how he addresses at times what is to come in your life, if you would only pay attention to what's being said and done.

I believe that it was the early part of November 2011 that Sis Coles and I had shared a conversation in which she talked about staying humble, fasting, and prayer, and I believe that in this day and age that we're living in, we all need to be doing all three.

Then at the nursing home on the 4th Sunday in November 2011, I spoke on seeking and searching for justice, not knowing that that very word would play an important part in my life in the following week and I am yet seeking and searching for justice, waiting for my change to come.

For never in my life have I been treated so badly and for so long, nine months is a mighty long time to me, and I recall saying in that message that one of the most basic needs in a human's life, is the need to be treated fairly.

But Paul lets us know that we need to endure hardness, which is to resist pressure in whatever form that it may come your way. Whether it's social pressure, peer pressure, or economic pressure

Or pressure of addictions, lusts, weights, or temptations.

And I think back to the week leading up to the candle light service   12/23/11

When things were so bad for me at work, and truth be told

 I wanted to lay hands on a couple of people and not pray but pound,

But I've learned down through the years the hard way

That the pen is mightier than the sword

And God dealt with me and I brought my flesh under subjection.

The Bible says to resist the devil and he will flee

Realizing that we all will face some difficult times,

We all will have our cross to carry.

So while I'm seeking and searching for justice

I am also doing a self check, so that I am not out of order.

For when you seek justice, you must be found to be just in your dealings with others

Just like the word of God says "those that desire to have friends must first be found to be friendly"

So I am examining myself, because I don't want anything hindering me from the truth.

And while I'm going through my trials, while I'm going through my tribulations,

It is extremely important that I stay focused on God, I have to stay prayed up, and I have to encourage myself and wait on my change to come.

For when you stay focused on your creator, God will give you a way of escape out of your trouble

For he is thinking about you and peace,

God says that he knows the thoughts that he has towards you, that of peace and not evil to give you an expected end.

Oh I thank God that he cares,

That he cares enough for us that we are on his mind.

I thank God that he sends encouragements to us

In various forms and at key times,

For while I was going through persecution,

While I was being mistreated and called awful names;

Being bombarded with injustice on every hand,

Even my friends that called or came by the job to see me, was being talked to nastily.

But God sent encouraging words; God sent encouraging words to me,

For one day while I was having a very trying day at work, I received a text message during that same work day, that brightened my whole day, and it simply said" You are my hero"

And not long after that on another occasion, I felt a light breeze kiss me on the cheek, and oh what an awesome mood that put me in, that God took time out to see about me.

God cares! . . . I know he cares;

Then I get to the candlelight service and God sends the scripture

PSALMS 18:28, "For thou wilt light my candle, the Lord my God will enlighten my darkness."

And I grabbed a hold of it that day

My second wind kicked in again, and I have a new found outlook on the situation.

God has rejuvenated me, no longer am I battle stressed

I am ready to defend and attack

Thank you Lord!!!

And I think on the word that says . . . God will not put more on you that you can bear

And sometimes I am like . . . God must think might highly of me, because I feel like I have the weight of the world on my shoulders and more just seem to keep coming.

Can anyone relate to that?

And I told the Lord all about it

And just like with Paul, I hear Jesus say "my grace is sufficient for you" you might not like where you are right now, but trust in me, trust in me, and watch me work in your life.

I hear Jesus say when he was talking to sons of Zebedee; he asked them are they willing to drink from the cup that I shall drink from, and be baptized with the baptism that I shall be baptized with? Then he said surely (indeed) you shall drink from this cup.

We as children of the most high God will have to drink the bitter contents of that cup.

Well . . . what is in the cup?

Attacks of the enemy are in the cup!

Persecution is in the cup!

Being lied on and talked about is in the cup!

Unfair treatment is in the cup!

Trials, tribulations, and tragedies are all in the cup!

And I want to know

How can you stand in the evil day, if you don't know how to respond to an attack?

The military soldier goes to basic training to learn the basics of soldiering and warfare, and it is not an option for them to choose

The spiritual soldier, the saint goes through new member's class in Sunday school to learn the basics of this faith lifestyle, but some view this as an option and don't attend that course regularly and fail to learn valuable golden nuggets of information to enhance their walk with God and to be able to combat the tactics of the enemy.

In the military, when you go to the firing range, they tell you to take all commands from the tower

Then they say that the firing range is ready, firers scan your lane

And what you are doing is being aware of your surroundings

Looking down a patch of field from 25 to 300 meters

Looking for an enemy target to pop up so that you can attempt to put a bullet in it,

Jesus says that man ought to watch and always pray.

So saints you too need to scan your lane,

For when the enemy rears its ugly head

Shoot him with the sixty six books and the Holy Spirit.

For that is your ammo,

For flesh cannot defeat spirit

If you're going to win any battles against Satan and his demons,

You're going to have to be in the spirit of God to do it.

My brothers and my sisters

The life of a soldier is not an easy life, but it is rewarding!

The life of a soldier is joyful over its relationship with its Lord!

The life of a soldier is about service and sacrifice!

Service to the people of God, and sacrifice . . . sometimes because of the same,

Isn't it ironic that sometimes the people that you help in this life?

Are the same ones that causes you the most grief

But the life of a soldier is one of perseverance!

Sometimes you just have to be able to brush your shoulders off

And don't stoop down to the dumb stuff

The life of a soldier is rooted in the word of God!

For a soldier knows" that I can do all things through Christ that strengthens me"

Child of God, I know that the enemy is not pleased

With the anointing that God has on my life,

And he is trying to derail me; he is trying to kill me.

The enemy is trying to derail and kill you because of your anointing,

Because of your gift, and your ministry

But God has got you covered

I hear Jesus say: Peter . . . . but not only Peter but "Word of Life" each and every one of you

Satan desires to have you,

That he may sift you as wheat

But I have prayed that your faith fails not

And I'm so thankful that Jesus prays for me that my faith fails not

For if you maintain your faith in God

You can expect miracles to come your way.

And as I close

I think back to my dad, when he suffered a life changing injury.

When his foot had got run over by a guy in a motorized wheel chair

And with poor circulation his injury didn't heal . . . having been in the hospital for months,

And day in and day out, he kept hearing the doctors give him a negative report,

We're going to have to amputate! . . .   We're going to have to take your leg!

Over and over that's what he heard

Not being able to care for himself like he used to,

Having to have someone else clean him up,

And I told him that it won't be like this always, you will be independent again.

And he just kept saying I hope so, I hope so,

And I would hear him say that he has to be out of the hospital by ten, ten:

That's 10/10/10   (October 10, 2010)

And at first I didn't understand, but I found out later that that's when his savings bonds matured

And that was enough motivation for him, to see him through his ordeal.

And now over a year later, at the age of 81,

The promise to walk again is in progress,

I tell you miracles do happen

And I'm so glad that we serve a true and living God,

That he honored the words that I spoke to my father in faith.

So a soldier must press on,

In spite of adversity,

In spite of negativity,

Child of God

Justice, righteous, and faith will prevail!

You have your marching orders!

Be just, be righteous, and have faith!

Soldiers of the Lord report!

You be encouraged

For God will . . . God will enlighten your darkness.

And when the light of the Lord comes in,

Every bit of darkness, every demonic force will have to flee.

And it's in my mind to strengthen my faith, and continue on the upward way,

For whatever God deems necessary for me to go through in this life,

No longer will I try to get out of it; no longer will I try to run from it

For I am assured that God will equip me for it.

And it's in my mind to soldier on, because I am a soldier of Jesus Christ

And if you soldier for the Kingdom of God,

You shall be blessed.

Thank You!

I pray that you have been blessed by reading this book!
Thank you for your love and support and most of all your prayers.

Contact the authors and leave a comment.

Aysha M. Youngblood-Moses
Email: amyoungblood73@yahoo.com

To JOHN & JAMILLA
THANK YOU FOR YOUR SUPPORT, LOVE
AND IN DESIGNING THE BOOK COVER
GOD BLESS

Harry W. Youngblood Jr.
Email: ubnice141965@yahoo.com

PSALMS 3 AND THE LAST VERSE!

Links: Word of Life Ministries: www.Johncalvin-wol.org

Put Some Honey On It

Harry W. Youngblood Jr.

OTHER BOOKS BY THE AUTHOR.

www.authorhouse.com